RUNNING THE DREAM

ONE SUMMER LIVING, TRAINING,
AND RACING WITH A TEAM OF
WORLD-CLASS RUNNERS HALF MY AGE

MATT FITZGERALD

PEGASUS BOOKS
NEW YORK LONDON

Pegasus Books, Ltd.
148 West 37th Street, 13th Floor
New York, NY 10018

First Pegasus Books paperback edition May 2021
First Pegasus Books cloth edition May 2020

Interior design by Maria Fernandez

The poem "Start Close In" by David Whyte is
reprinted with permission from Many Rivers Press.

David Whyte, "Star Close In," from *David Whyte: Essentials*
© Many Rivers Press, Langley, WA USA.

Library of Congress Cataloging-in-Publication Data is available.

ISBN: 978-1-64313-762-9

10 9 8 7 6 5 4 3 2 1

Printed in the United States of America
Distributed by Simon & Schuster
www.pegasusbooks.com

For Mom

CONTENTS

There's something about living the grind and getting up in the morning and putting in the mileage and running the workouts and doing all that stuff that is . . . just so *satisfying*. There's something about getting the absolute most out of yourself that I think is admirable, regardless of where the ceiling is.

—Nick Hilton, an unsponsored 2:16 marathoner, speaking to letsrun.com in 2018, six years after he packed all his possessions into a Volkswagen and moved to Flagstaff

JULY

93 Days to Chicago

Nine sets of (mostly nonmatching) running shorts and tops. A rainbow assortment of running socks. Running tights in two thicknesses and an old pair of half-tights worn down to gossamer in the seat area by unnumbered washings. Running gloves, running arm warmers, and a thermal running hat for cold days and a performance rain jacket for wet ones. A couple of warm-up suits. Three pairs of size 11.5 running shoes. Eight or nine running-themed T-shirts, some of them mementos of past races, others bearing the Hoka One One Northern Arizona Elite professional running team logo. Seven pairs of Runderwear brand athletic boxer briefs.

I stuffed these items into the larger of two well-traveled Samsonite suitcases when I packed last night, having waited until my afternoon run was out of the way to do laundry. Into the smaller suitcase went an assortment of other essentials: energy gel packets, gel flasks, a canister of powdered sports drink mix, effervescent electrolyte tablets, a handheld drink flask, energy chews, energy bars, a hydration belt, an iPhone armband, wireless sport headphones, sport sunglasses, a roll of kinesiology tape, and a GPS running watch with charging cord.

Lacking both space and need for much else in the Fun Mobile (my wife Nataki's name for our Mazda crossover), I crammed the gaps around our bags this morning with a few more items I wouldn't dream of leaving behind, including compression boots for post-run recovery and a vibrating foam roller for the same use. Oh, and our dog, Queenie.

We hit the road at eight o'clock, right on schedule, traveling precisely one block before I realized I'd forgotten my driving shades. Annoyed beyond measure (time waste is a trigger for me), I pulled a violent one-eighty and sped back to the house, stopping hard at the curb instead of pulling into the driveway. I'd just succeeded in fumbling the house key into the front door lock when, hearing my name, I turned around to see Nataki gesturing casually in the direction of the garage, which was blocked from my view by a corner of the house.

"Garage is open," she said.

Moments later I was back in the driver seat, buckling up with the forgotten eyewear perched on the crown of my head.

"We dodged a bullet there," I said.

Indeed we had. Nataki and I were leaving home for thirteen weeks, an entire summer, to fulfill a dream—*my* dream—of living the life of a professional runner. That's an awful long time to leave your garage door open.

Driving off again, I pressed the Fun Mobile's voice command button and recited the home address of Matt Llano, a member of NAZ Elite and my teammate for the next three months. A vaguely feminine humanoid voice informed me that the drive from Oakdale, California, to Flagstaff, Arizona, would take ten hours, thirty-one minutes. Matt rents out rooms in his house to athletes visiting Flagstaff for high-altitude training. Most if not all these folks are not middle-age amateurs like me but real pros like Sally Kipyego, an Olympic silver medalist from Kenya, who recently slept in the same bed Nataki and I will share during our stay. It is unlikely that a slower runner than me has ever lain on that particular mattress.

Obeying our android guide, I headed south on Geer Road—a two-lane country highway choked with trucks driven by agricultural workers on their way to an honest day's labor—to Turlock, where we picked up Route 99 and continued south through the Central California eyesores of Fresno and Visalia and Bakersfield before bending east. The dashboard temperature reading rose steadily as we pressed inland, peaking at an astonishing 122 degrees in the town of Needles on the Arizona border. We then began to climb, reaching 3,000 feet on the approach to Kingman, 4,000 feet near the Yavapai County line, and 5,000 feet as we skirted Seligman, the mercury falling in proportion to the Fun Mobile's ascension. Between Ash Fork (5,160 feet) and Williams (6,766 feet), our rocky brown surroundings gave way to the lush verdure of the Coconino National Forest, in which Flagstaff nestles like a jewel on a bed of green velvet. A pale late afternoon sun was dipping languorously behind us when we hit the city limit. Canceling the navigation, I skipped Matt's exit, took the next one, and cruised along South Milton Road, Flagstaff's main drag, until I spied a Chili's restaurant on the right. Minutes later we were enjoying an early dinner of burgers and fries (and beer, for me)—a sort of last hurrah. For the next ninety-three days, until the Chicago Marathon on October 8, I will do everything the real pros do and make every sacrifice they make in pursuit of the absolute limit of their God-given abilities, dietary sacrifices not excepted. From what I've heard, Matt Llano himself eats like a saint and has never tasted alcohol in his entire life. I don't know if I can match his standard, but I'm going to try.

At six o'clock, our promised arrival time, I rang the doorbell of a newish home in the upscale Ponderosa Trails neighborhood, sucking on a breath mint. The door swung open and Matt appeared at the threshold. If I hadn't known he was a world-class runner, I would have guessed it just by looking at him. His twenty-eight-year-old body has an avian economy, a built-for-flight appearance that is only hinted at by the talc of the tape: five-foot-nine, 125 pounds, 6 percent body fat.

"You made it!" he said, exposing a set of almost luminously white chompers. "Come on in."

"We brought pluots!" I blurted in reply, handing Matt two large cloth bags filled with the ripe fruit Nataki and I had pulled off a tree in our backyard yesterday. Taken aback by the near-industrial volume of produce being foisted on him, Matt stared at the bags for an awkward second before accepting them.

"I love pluots!" he said, recovering. "I'll do some baking with these."

Matt led us upstairs and showed us our room, which we discovered to be about half again the size of our own master suite. I hauled our stuff in from the car while Nataki went to work unpacking and arranging. When this was done, I went downstairs to be sociable. I found Matt sitting at his kitchen breakfast bar eating a salad of kale, broccoli, shaved Brussels sprouts, cabbage, radicchio, avocado, cranberries, roasted pumpkin seeds, and apple cider vinaigrette topped with roasted chicken breast—a fairly typical dinner, he explained. Also present were his full-time housemate, Jason Blair, a local policeman with whom Matt went to high school in Maryland, and Jen Spieldenner, a professional triathlete from Ohio currently occupying a smaller guest bedroom on the first floor.

"What does Ben have you doing the next few days?" Matt asked.

Ben Rosario is the coach of NAZ Elite and a big reason I'm here, having responded with a surprisingly unhesitating "yes" when I emailed him eight months ago to ask if I could spend a summer as an unofficial member of his team and write about the experience.

"Not much," I grumbled. "No run today, four miles tomorrow, six miles Sunday, and then I start running with the team."

"That's good, though," Jen said. "Seven thousand feet is no joke. You have to ease into training at this elevation. Even if you feel good, it's important to hold back. I made the mistake of doing too much too soon the first time I came here, and I dug a hole for myself that I never got out of."

"It's not just your running that's affected," Matt added. "When I moved here in 2011, my appetite went crazy. I would lie awake at night in the fetal position, miserable, too hungry to sleep and too exhausted to go upstairs to the kitchen for food."

"And if you have any kind of open wound, it will never heal," Jen piled on. "Last year when I came here, I had a sore on my lip. When I went home after three weeks, I still had it."

Suddenly sleepy, I said goodnight to my new friends and shuffled off to bed, wondering what the hell I've gotten myself into.

92 Days to Chicago

Our first full day in Flagstaff got off to a low-key start, with a little more unpacking and arranging, a quick trip to Save Mart for groceries, and a bit of neighborhood exploration with Queenie. At 11:30 Nataki and I drove to the north side of town for a working lunch with Ben Rosario at Kickstand Kafé, a coffeehouse that, according to Matt, my new coach likes to use as an office.

While the three of us waited in line to order, I studied a paper menu intensively, asking myself what a real professional runner would select. Having seen Matt breakfast on a "smoothie bowl" that contained almond milk, coconut water, acai, blueberries, blackberries, raspberries, beet, banana, kiwi, dragon fruit, granola, honey, coconut, almond butter, and organic vanilla protein powder, I decided on the grilled vegetable burrito and the kale salad, splitting the latter with Nataki, who also ordered a turkey panini. Ben, who retired from professional running several years ago, went for the chorizo burrito. I paid for everything and we found seats at a small wooden table.

"So, have you run yet?" Ben asked.

I'd met Ben twice before and had seen him in a million online videos, but I was struck anew by the boyishness of his appearance. Nine years my junior, he looks even younger, with an elfin sparkle in his eyes and a mop of unruly brown curls spilling from under an ever-present NAZ Elite trucker hat.

"Yeah, about that," I answered, smiling guiltily.

"Uh-oh," Ben said. "What happened?"

What happened, I proceeded to explain, was that I left the front door to Matt's house open a split second too long (something my host had warned me against doing) when Nataki and I returned from walking Queenie this morning, and Matt's dog, Harlow, bolted. Panicked, I scrambled after the animal, a vigorous two-year-old rescue dog of unknown pedigree but of undeniable swiftness. To my horror, she made straight for the main road, but it was lightly trafficked, thank God, and she managed to cross unharmed to the residential neighborhood that lay opposite. Despite putting everything I had into my pursuit of the rogue mutt, I continued to lose ground until she stopped and turned to monitor my approach, head lowered tauntingly.

Harlow let me get within twenty feet of her before taking off again, forcing me to renew the chase. This little game continued until we were nearly half a mile from the house and I was about ready to keel over, my esophagus raked raw by oxygen-poor air, at which point my canine tormenter showed mercy and let me seize her by the collar.

"Anyway, so much for easing into life at 7,000 feet," I concluded.

"Lesson learned, I'm sure," Ben said. He chuckled lightly, then turned serious. "Now let's talk about the road ahead. The main thing I want you to take away from this meeting is a general understanding of what the next three months are going to look like. What you'll see over the first few weeks is a lot of variety. It'll be an eclectic blend of workouts. Nothing will be terribly difficult because what I've found is that if you start doing the marathon-specific work too far out, you get stale.

"Around the middle of August," Ben resumed after pausing to gnaw his burrito, "which is eight weeks out from Chicago, we'll switch it up. From that point on you'll do pretty much nothing *but* marathon-specific stuff, because the marathon really only has that one zone that you're in the whole way through, so you don't need all those other tools in your toolbox. You just need to be really efficient at a high aerobic intensity. Any questions?"

"Can we talk about my goal?" I said. "I know it's early, and we have no idea yet how I will adapt to the altitude and the training and everything else. But I'd at least like to get the conversation started."

"Go ahead, give me a number."

"I'll give you a bunch of numbers," I said. "I'm forty-six years old. I started running when I was eleven. I've completed forty marathons, give or take, over the past eighteen years. My best time is 2:41:29, which I ran nine years ago, when I was thirty-seven. My most recent marathon was in Eugene in May, and my time there was 2:49:14. It's a safe bet that no runner in history who has run as many marathons as I have over such a long period of time and whose best marathon is so far past has ever set a new personal best at my age. I've read the science, and I have no illusions about how aging affects performance. Did you know that the marathon world record for forty-six-year-olds is *nine minutes* slower than the marathon world record for thirty-seven-year-olds? I've actually done pretty well to have slowed down by only eight minutes."

"But . . ." Ben said.

"But my heart says that maybe it's *not* impossible for me to still run a faster marathon. Can I find eight minutes of improvement in this environment? Let's say training at high altitude gives me one minute, running more miles gives me another minute, losing a few pounds gives me another minute . . . who knows?"

The truth is that I did not want to run 2:41:28—a nominal personal best—or even 2:40. I wanted to run 2:39, but I kept this information to myself. For one thing, I didn't want to burden Ben with such an outlandish ambition. But the main reason was that I just didn't know how to articulate what this number—this long-sought, never-attained goal turned symbol of unfulfilled potential—means to me.

"I would say this," Ben said. "To start with 2:45 in your mind would be very reasonable. If that's where you end up, great. If we find ourselves pleasantly surprised as we move along, even better. My philosophy—and this is the philosophy of any decent coach—is that you base the training not on the athlete's goal but on his most recent fitness, which for you is 2:49. Then, if the athlete is hitting all the targets, you raise the bar. You don't do the opposite and start writing workouts for a 2:41 guy when he's not a 2:41 guy currently. Make sense?"

"I am clay," I said, spreading my hands. "Mold me."

90 Days to Chicago

On Sundays Coach Ben sends out a group email to the full NAZ Elite roster and other affiliated parties (Ben's wife, Jen, who assists the team; agent Josh Cox; a couple of executives at team sponsor Hoka; any interns currently with the group). Bearing the invariant subject line "THIS

WEEK," it contains news and announcements, housekeeping items, and a schedule for the next seven days. Yesterday's missive began as follows:

> First of all . . . welcome to the team, Matt Fitzgerald! Matt arrived Friday night, nearly lost Matt's dog on Saturday, and will join us officially beginning tomorrow. He'll be with us all the way through the Chicago Marathon, so we'll have plenty of time to get to know him. Matt—looking forward to having you.

Scrolling down to the schedule, I found my name on a list of runners instructed to meet at a place called Walnut Canyon at 8:30 this morning for an easy run—my first session with the real pros. Last night I found Matt in the kitchen baking a tart with some of the pluots Nataki and I brought from home and asked him where Walnut Canyon was, explaining that hitching a ride with him was not an option because I had to get a blood draw at 7:00 and intended to head straight from the lab to the meetup. Matt promised to drop a pin for me.

"There's no address, so it might not get you to the exact location, but it will get you close," he said. "Just look for the first parking area on the left."

Arriving in the vicinity a few minutes early, I managed to find *a* parking area near Matt's pin. I pulled in and was just about to cut the engine and settle in with Nataki and Queenie to wait for others to show up when a gray Subaru Outback pulled in next to us. The driver's window slid down to reveal the smiling face of Scott Fauble, a 25-year-old Colorado native who finished fourth for NAZ Elite in the 2016 U.S. Olympic Trials Men's 10,000m, just missing out on qualifying for the Rio Olympics.

"I saw you pass me on the highway," he said. "You went too far. Follow me."

As we trailed Scott back in the direction we'd come from, I wondered briefly how the heck he'd known who I was before remembering the NAZ Elite sticker I'd proudly slapped on the rear bumper of the Fun Mobile before leaving California.

When we got back to the parking area I was supposed to have stopped at, Matt was there, just emerging from a shiny black Range Rover Evoque.

"Are you ready for this?" Nataki asked.

"Honestly, I have no idea," I said.

With this rousing battle cry, I unbuckled and joined my new teammates in the mountain-fresh air of Walnut Canyon, the kind of air you instinctively draw in through your nose and exhale in a giant sigh. *Aaah!* I shook Scott's hand, made small talk, and then looked on awkwardly as he and Matt withdrew exercise mats from their vehicles and performed a series of stretches and muscle activation exercises that, lacking the required tools, I could not make myself less conspicuous by emulating.

Matt began with an unfamiliar version of a familiar hip flexor stretch. Assuming a kneeling position, he looped a long elastic strap around the knee of the front leg and pulled the ends toward his body with his hands while pressing his pelvis forward.

"What's the strap for?" I asked.

"It allows the stretch to target the hip flexors more effectively," he said.

Matt has had two hip surgeries, one on each side, and is still recovering from the second, which was done to repair a torn labrum in the left hip suffered during last year's New York City Marathon. He and Scott are now training for the Frankfurt Marathon, which falls four weeks after Chicago.

"I have super tight hip flexors," I volunteered.

"Here, try it," Matt said, handing me the strap.

I took his place on the mat and did as he had done. Sure enough, I felt a stronger tug in the pocket area of the hip than I feel with the strapless version of the exercise.

"See?" I called out to Nataki. "I learned something already!"

Other runners were now arriving, producing mats of their own, and limbering up. I recognized most of them. Stephanie Bruce was the top non-African-born finisher at this year's World Cross Country Championships. Her husband, Ben Bruce, at thirty-four the oldest member of NAZ Elite, has finished tenth, ninth, eighth, seventh, sixth, fifth, fourth, third, and second in various national championship events—but never first. Amy Van Alstine, who is five years younger than Ben, has won a couple of national championships in cross country. Aaron "Brauny" Braun is a former national road racing champion and is also training for the Chicago Marathon. Scott Smith, who splits time between Los Angeles and Flagstaff, ran a 1:02:34 half marathon last year and will race Frankfurt alongside Matt and Scott Fauble (usually addressed as "Faubs" to avoid confusion).

Not present were Futsum Zeinasellassie, a four-time NCAA Division I All-American at Flagstaff's own Northern Arizona University, who is taking a break after the USATF Outdoor Championships; Martin Hehir, a satellite member of NAZ Elite who is about to start medical school in Philadelphia; Rochelle Kanuho, a 1:11 half marathoner; Craig Lutz, a cross country national champion at both the high-school and professional levels; and Kellyn Taylor, a 2:28 marathoner who is in Phoenix this week taking EMT classes as part of her training to become a professional firefighter.

When Coach Ben arrived, he welcomed me on behalf of the team and asked if I had any questions.

"I'd just like to say that if I have trouble keeping up with you guys today it's only because I've lost a lot of blood," I said, pointing at a piece of gauze affixed to the crook of my left elbow with a strip of blue medical tape.

The blood draw had been arranged by Wes Gregg, a chiropractor and strength and conditioning coach who, in partnership with his brother AJ, oversees chiropractic, physical therapy, dietetic, strength training, sports psychology, and physiological testing services for NAZ Elite at a local facility called Hypo2 Sport. The point of training at high altitude as a runner is to stimulate the body to produce more red blood cells, thereby increasing the oxygen-carrying capacity of the blood and boosting sea-level performance. The body needs an adequate supply of iron to manufacture new red blood cells, so it's important for runners to monitor their iron levels while training in the mountains. My blood will be tested for ferritin (an iron-storing protein), hemoglobin (the oxygen-carrying component of red blood cells), and hematocrit (a measure of red blood cell concentration), among other components. Four weeks from now, Wes will order a second draw to see if altitude training is actually working for me (i.e., if my hemoglobin and hematocrit numbers have increased) and if my iron levels are keeping up with the demand.

Mats and straps went back into vehicles, outer layers were stripped off, and the run began. I kissed Nataki (who doesn't run) and fell in with the group, pleasantly surprised by the leisureliness of the initial pace. Stephanie (or Steph, as everyone calls her), who has two young boys, made a maternal effort to hang back with me and engage me in conversation.

"So, what's your goal for Chicago?" she asked.

"Well, my last marathon was a 2:49, so I guess anything better than that would count as a success," I lied.

After half a mile we turned off the flat gravel road we'd started on and picked up a trailhead that led us into thick forest, where the terrain was much more challenging—twisting, rugged, hilly—and the pace that seemed comfortable to me before no longer did. I fell behind with Coach Ben, whose own elite racing days were cut short by a chronic hamstring injury that even now limits him to a few easy miles here and there. We talked all things running until my watch said I'd covered three miles, at which point we turned around. Our vehicles had just come into view when our conversation lulled, freeing my attention to swing outward to our surroundings: sunshine dappling the smooth surface of a duck pond to my left, the majestic San Francisco Peaks looming in the distance, fragrant alpine air filling my lungs, soft dirt underfoot.

I found Nataki sitting on a bench contemplating the water, Queenie at her feet.

"How did it go?" my wife asked.

I stole a sidelong glance at Coach Ben to make sure he was out of earshot.

"I can't believe I'm getting away with this," I said.

89 Days to Chicago

Matt Llano spends more time in his kitchen than other people spend in front of their televisions. Two days ago, I came back to the house from a six-mile run to find him on galley duty once again, making bison balls. We had a brief exchange while I fetched a glass from a cupboard, filled it with water, and drank (my thirst has been out of control ever since I got here). Matt asked me which route I'd taken and I told him. He then asked me when I was going to do my first workout and I stared at him like he was an idiot. *Dude, I'm standing right in front of you wearing sweaty workout clothes!* I didn't actually say these words, but my eyes did. Then I realized I was the idiot.

In the parlance of elite-level distance running, a workout is a hard run that includes efforts at high intensity. Slow-and-steady runs like the one I'd just completed are not workouts but *easy runs,* or just *runs.* Like most recreational runners, I tend to use the words *run* and *workout* interchangeably, a habit I quietly vowed to break myself of as Matt awaited my answer.

"Tuesday," I answered a second late. "Coach Ben's given me a six-mile steady state."

There's another one: *steady state.* Few recreational runners employ this term, which any pro runner can tell you refers to a workout featuring an extended segment at or near marathon effort. At sea level, *marathon effort* is equal to *marathon pace,* but at high altitude it's a little slower. Coach Ben uses a calculator designed by the legendary exercise physiologist and running coach Jack Daniels to convert sea-level paces to their 7,000-foot equivalents. The target pace he gave me for today's steady state was 6:50 per mile, which, according to Daniels, is the Flagstaff-elevation equivalent of 6:30 per mile at sea level, or about the pace I averaged in the Eugene Marathon nine weeks ago. Ben had told me my early workouts here would be fairly easy, and I expected this one to be an outright snoozer.

We met at Buffalo Park, a 215-acre runner's paradise of groomed dirt trails that wind through sprawling meadows offering spectacular views of the Dry Lake Hills, the San Francisco Peaks, and Mount Elden. Matt, Faubs, and I were again the first runners to arrive. This time, however, I did not stand around like a dork watching them stretch but joined them, using an exercise mat and a resistance strap I bought yesterday from the local Big 5. Catching Faubs looking, I gave him a wink. We were soon joined by Scott Smith, Brauny, and Ian Frazier, a runner from University of Central Missouri who was interning with NAZ Elite for the summer.

We warmed up with a tour of the two-mile loop I'd be using for my workout while my teammates did hill circuits on a different loop. They fed me helpful tips as we went, showing me the one fork in the trail where I might take a wrong turn if I wasn't paying attention and where to "bank time" by running ahead of my target pace so that the lung-busting climb at the end of the loop didn't put me behind. Glancing at my watch, I saw that our current pace was 7:05 per mile—just fifteen seconds slower than my steady-state pace. The others found this amusing.

"One man's warm-up is another man's steady state," Faubs said. "That's okay."

When we got back to our starting point, the real pros swapped their bulky trainers for ultralight Hoka Tracer racing flats and performed a rote series of bounding and skipping drills and short, relaxed sprints, known as strides. Again I marked myself as the new guy by keeping my trainers on (I don't own racing flats) and skipping the drills, which looked a bit too much like dancing for my comfort. Preliminaries complete, Brauny, Faubs, Matt, and Scott left for the hilly loop.

"Are you ready to go?" Coach Ben asked.

I looked from Ben to the receding backs of the athletes who were actually getting paid for this and back to Ben.

"Aren't you going with them?"

"Ian has them covered," Ben said. "I want to get your splits."

I came to Flagstaff with certain expectations. Getting preferential coaching treatment—even if only in the beginning—was not one of them. Speechless, I followed Ben to the start of the loop. Launching on his cue, I accelerated to a pace that seemed about right and then used my watch to fine tune until I was locked in at 6:50 per mile. Nothing to it.

All of a sudden I felt as though I were breathing through a straw. A blind panic seized me, the kind of whole-body freak-out you experience when an improperly chewed morsel lodges in your throat and you know you're going to die. I told myself to relax, understanding on some level that what

I was experiencing was probably just a primal suffocation reflex triggered by an unfamiliar mismatch between my body's demand for oxygen and the supply it was getting from the thin air surrounding me, and the feeling soon went away.

By the time I reached the big hill, I was ahead of pace and could afford to cruise it. Coach Ben stood near the summit, calling out numbers. The moment I passed him, he sprinted along a diagonal and met me again at the end of the loop, where he announced my split time and told me I was looking good. I giggled in response. Ben Rosario, the guy from the online videos and the podcast interviews and the magazine articles and the occasional TV appearance, scrambling around like a water boy in the service of me, nobody. It didn't seem real.

The next two loops were free of drama. I jogged one last loop to cool down and returned to the parking lot just as the big boys were returning from the opposite direction.

"How was it?" Faubs called out from twenty yards away.

"I survived," I called back.

"Hey, some days that's all you can ask for."

87 Days to Chicago

When I first heard mention of the Bagel Run, I mistakenly interpreted the "bagel" part literally and the "run" part nonliterally, assuming the name referred to some sort of team errand to procure Jewish donuts. In fact, I now know, the Bagel Run is an all-comers group run that begins every Thursday at 8 A.M. at the corner of Beaver Street and Phoenix Avenue, outside Biff's Bagels. Started many years ago by Mike Smith, who had previously founded Team Run Flagstaff, the city's big running club, and is now the cross country and track coach at Northern Arizona University, the event attracts a mixture of elites (2:11 marathoner Nick Arciniaga is a fixture) and serious amateurs. Coach Ben, who likes his runners to mingle with the broader local running population, always puts it on the schedules of at least a few NAZ Elite members, and I found it on my schedule this morning.

Ben himself shows up when time permits and did so today. I found a place next to him at the back of a group of some two dozen as we headed southward from Biff's, threading through the NAU campus and onto the Urban Trail, a fifty-six-mile network of gravel paths that, no matter where you happen to be in Flagstaff, you're always near. After three miles, far behind the others now and engrossed in a debate about the relative merits of Tim Noakes's central governor theory of endurance performance and Samuele Marcora's psychobiological model of the same, we turned around.

On the way back, we were caught from behind by a couple of runners who'd taken off at the head of the group. One of them, olive-skinned and lightly bearded, greeted Ben familiarly. He bore a striking resemblance to David Torrence, one of my favorite pro runners. Then it hit me: Given the context, he just might be David Torrence! My heart fluttered. I like David because he's a late bloomer—a B-level collegiate miler at Berkeley who made his first Olympic team (representing Peru) at age thirty—and because he races with childlike gusto, sometimes rocking a fauxhawk. I'll never forget his professional debut at 5000 meters in 2012, a race in which Lopez Lomong miscounted the laps and started kicking with two laps to go and David, who had not miscounted, went with him anyway, insanely, knowing full well it was suicidal but unable to help himself.

"Don't tell me you guys have run eight miles in the time it's taken us to run six!" I said, trying to lure David (or his doppelgänger) into conversation, so I could claim I've met him.

"Of course not," said the guy who was almost certainly David Torrence. "More like *ten* miles!"

I laughed louder than was warranted. The object of my fawning then put the back of a hand to the side of his mouth and stage-whispered to his friend, "That David Torrence is such an asshole!"

That asshole is *David Torrence!*

Upon returning to the Fun Mobile, where Nataki and Queenie were chilling after their morning walk, I checked the time and decided it wasn't worth the bother to drive back to Matt's place for a quick scrub and wardrobe change before the eleven o'clock team strength workout at Hypo2, another Thursday ritual for NAZ Elite. So instead my wife and I grabbed a second breakfast (or early lunch, or whatever) at Biff's. Channeling my inner Matt Llano, I ordered a veggie deluxe bagel sandwich on whole wheat, no cheese. Six days into this experiment, I've already dropped four pounds. Whether this was because of my efforts to cut back on cheese, chocolate, and beer or because, as Scott Fauble insists, *everyone* loses a few pounds initially in Flagstaff I can't say.

The address Siri led me to after the meal turned out to be shared by a pair of unmarked buildings that lay on opposite sides of an access road in a small business park near Buffalo Park. It took a seeming eternity to identify which building housed Hypo2 and a second eternity to find an unlocked door, and by the time I'd found the entrance and negotiated the facility's mazelike hallways to the strength and conditioning room, I was several minutes late and my teammates were already working out. Seeing me enter, Coach Ben flagged me down and introduced me to Wes Gregg, who was younger than I'd pictured him, probably late twenties.

"I've got the results from your blood work," he said, handing me a sheet of paper. I scanned it in the expectation of seeing interesting facts about my iron level but found only a blur of nonsense words ("basophils") and crazy alphanumerical codes ("x10E3/uL") that meant nothing to me.

"Just give it to me straight, doc," I said. "Am I dying?"

"No, you're not dying," Wes laughed. "Your hemoglobin and hematocrit numbers are fine. But your ferritin is lower than I would like it to be." He placed the tip of an index finger near the bottom of the page. "You're at forty-five nanograms per milliliter, which is technically normal, but I prefer to see male runners stay above fifty."

"I feel a lot better since I started supplementing," I said. "I must have been *really* low before."

On Coach Ben's advice, I had put myself on a daily iron regimen in advance of coming to Flagstaff.

"Ultimately, it's how you feel that matters most," Wes said. "We'll keep an eye on that and order another test in a few weeks to be safe."

We were joined now by a square-chinned man who had the ramrod-straight posture and unexcitable bearing of a commando—Wes's older brother and business partner, AJ.

"I've got a workout for you," he said quietly, presenting me with another sheet of paper as though it were a costly gift.

I scanned this second item in the same manner as the first and was chagrined to discover that its contents were nearly as indecipherable.

"What does 'SL RDL' stand for?" I asked.

"Single-leg reverse deadlift," AJ said.

I gave him a blank look. He snatched a dumbbell from a rack, balanced on his right foot, and tilted his trunk forward, reaching toward the toe of his right shoe while kicking the left leg back. It looked easy enough, but when I tried it, I lost my balance almost immediately and stumbled forward like an overladen backpacker tripping over an exposed root. Conscious of AJ's attention, I hastily reset myself and tried again, only to stagger sideways this time. It took me several minutes to complete ten proper repetitions on each foot.

"You probably think I haven't lifted a weight in my life," I said to AJ, flushing. "Truth is, I'm in the gym three times every week!"

"We do things a little differently than most runners," AJ said. "A lot of single-leg stuff, balance work, a big focus on those smaller stabilizer muscles that traditional exercises miss. If you're not used to that kind of stuff, it will take a little time to get proficient."

I consulted my workout sheet and was relieved to see a familiar exercise next on the list: side planks.

"How long do you normally hold them?" AJ asked.

"Thirty seconds," I said.

"Let's try sixty," AJ said.

It turns out that a sixty-second side plank is twice as difficult as a thirty-second side plank. A muscle I didn't even know existed cramped along my ribcage as I adjusted my form in obedience to AJ's corrections ("Don't stack your feet," "Press those hips forward," "You're sagging again"), each of which served to make the exercise even harder. Veronica, an intern, timed me, and when she delivered the welcome news that a minute was up, I collapsed to the floor.

"Let's try ninety," AJ said.

Forty-five seconds into set number two, my body was shuddering like a taut clothesline in a gale, and by seventy-five seconds I was flapping like the Tacoma Narrows Bridge in that famous 1940 disaster video—or so I felt. AJ put a fist to his mouth to hide a smile.

On and on it went, embarrassment piling on top of embarrassment, like some kind of fitness cult hazing. When I completed my last set of "stirring the pot," an abdominal exercise every bit as muscle-searing as a ninety-second side plank, it was well past noon and I was the only runner left in the room—except for David Torrence, who, though not a member of NAZ Elite, has the same shoe sponsor and often works out with the team when he comes to Flagstaff from his home in Scottsdale for a dose of altitude. David had spent the past hour doing barbell back squats with seemingly impossible amounts of weight for a man of such pixieish stature.

Recognizing me from our Bagel Run encounter, he approached with a hand out.

"Hi, I'm David," he said.

"I know who you are," I said. "I'm Matt."

"How long have you been with the team?" he asked.

"Well, I'm not really with the team," I said hastily, conscious of the gray hair at my temples. "My real job is writing about running. Coach Ben's letting me tag along for a few months to see what the pro lifestyle does for a mere mortal."

"Wait—what's your last name?"

I told him.

"I've read some of your stuff!" David exclaimed. "You wrote *Racing Weight*, right? I'm a big fan of your work."

I sensed that David was laying it on thick, perhaps having caught a glimpse or two of the humiliation I'd just endured and deciding to prop up my ego with a little compassionate flattery. If so, it worked.

I drove back to Matt's place with all the windows of the Fun Mobile rolled down and the sunroof open so that Nataki and I didn't suffocate in the locker room smell emanating from my skin. Still, it didn't seem worth the bother to shower and change before my afternoon run, an easy solo four-miler, so I didn't. I should make a note to ask someone if exercising three times in the same clothes is normal for real pro runners.

86 Days to Chicago

Hattie Greene is a mile-long loop of smooth and level asphalt that lies curled inside a wealthy private community occupying former pastureland in north Flagstaff, acreage once owned by the road's namesake, a celebrated archaeologist, conservationist, and poetess who lived from 1880 to 1962. Having discovered it only recently despite living close by, Coach Ben, who collects such locations for use in workouts, asked the team to meet there this morning for a "log speed" session, as he called it, which, for me, would consist of sixteen times 300 meters at roughly 5K race pace (adjusted for altitude) with 200-meter jogs between reps. Ben was measuring the course with a hand wheel, placing cones at 100-meter intervals, when I rolled in with Nataki and Queenie, catching sight of a family of deer across a broad field as I parked the Fun Mobile behind Ben's Honda Pilot. It was then I realized I'd left my watch back at Matt's place.

"Not a problem," Ben said when I confessed the rookie lapse. "Eric Fernandez is coming out to pace you. He'll be your watch today."

I had met Eric once before, in Sacramento, on the eve of last year's California International Marathon (CIM). I was huddling with Coach Ben and Josh Cox, the sports agent who represents NAZ Elite, at a downtown

Starbucks, working through the logistics of my plan to join the team the following summer, when Eric passed through on his way back to the Sheraton Grand to put his feet up and kill the remaining hours before the race, which I was also running. I saw him again the next morning, looking focused and ready at the start line. And ready he was. While I rode the struggle bus far, far behind him, somehow hitting the wall at *three miles* and staggering to the finish fifteen minutes off my goal time, Eric blitzed a 2:14:09, good for fourth place, an auspicious marathon debut after years of battling injuries.

Alas, Eric had only just begun to ramp up for his next marathon when he suffered yet another stress fracture and decided enough was enough. Just twenty-seven years old, he pulled the plug on his pro running career, trading the roads for the weight room in an effort to bulk up. But, as Coach Ben explained to me while we awaited his arrival at Hattie Greene, Eric remains under contract with the team until the end of the year and has agreed to earn his last few scraps of remuneration by performing such unglamorous tasks as keeping middle-age fake pro runners company during workouts.

The Eric Fernandez who unfolded himself from a silver Jeep Patriot minutes later scarcely resembled the one I met in Sacramento. Dressed in baggy gym shorts and an old Hoka tank top stretched tight across a bench-press-inflated chest, he appeared even taller than the six-foot-three stature that had earned him the nickname "Big Dog" (and had probably contributed to his susceptibility to foot injuries).

"Wow!" I said, shaking his hand while taking note of a University of Arkansas Razorback shoulder tattoo. "If I didn't know differently, I would never guess you used to be a runner."

"Really?" Eric said, glowing. "Don't say that if you don't mean it!"

We warmed up with Amy Van Alstine, the three of us following well behind Aaron, Faubs, and Scott on an overgrown dirt rut that spit us out at Buffalo Park, where we took turns using the portable toilets before heading back to Hattie Greene. We returned to find Coach Ben engrossed in an animated conversation with an older resident who, we were soon apprised, had been driving by when he spotted the cones and our parked vehicles and stopped to see if there was anything he could do to ruin our morning. We waited at a respectful distance until the busybody had climbed back into his van and pulled away.

"Bad news," Ben reported. "We've been kicked out. Private property, liability issue, blah blah blah."

"And that, in a nutshell, is the difference between professional running and every other professional sport," Eric said for my benefit.

With a mixture of grumbling and snickering, we piled into our cars and trucks and decamped, scooching a couple of miles south to Ben's own neighborhood, where our coach hastily repeated the whole business of measuring and placing cones while the rest of us repeated our warm-ups.

"I may need as much help with counting as I do with pacing," I told Eric at the start cone. He laughed politely.

"I'm serious!" I said. "I've never done sixteen repetitions of *anything* before."

Coach Ben sent us off with a two-letter command. The big boys shot ahead immediately, chasing a target time of fifty-one seconds per 300 meters to my sixty-three seconds. Amy, meanwhile, hampered by a nagging pelvis injury, pulled away more gradually, the distance separating her from Big Dog and me remaining small enough to create a certain awkwardness—two heavy-breathing dudes stalking a woman in bun huggers.

"Don't mind us, little lady!" Eric bellowed near the end of the rep.

I wasn't the only one feeling a little icky, evidently. Amy showed us her right middle finger and I stopped worrying.

We hit the finish cone and slowed to a jog.

"How many was that?" I joked.

"I'm not sure," Eric said. "Number four, I think."

We continued to banter in this manner as we ticked off the succeeding reps, Big Dog appearing to be as little challenged by the workout as I was despite his having run no more than a mile at a time in several weeks. Midway through the final rep, he goaded me into squealing the ridiculous battle cry of Razorback football fans—"Woo pig sooie!"—as we finished.

The outburst got exactly the response I expected from Amy, Brauny, and the two Scotts: a combination of eye rolls and head shakes that suggested a weary familiarity with their former teammate's over-the-top pride in his alma mater.

"How was it?" Coach Ben asked, shadowing me as I walked to the Fun Mobile to grab my water bottle.

"I liked it," I said. "It was different for me. Whenever I do a workout at this intensity on my own, it's always longer efforts—600s, 800s—and it's always hard. But I feel good now. The shorter reps made it more manageable to do the same total amount of work at the same effort level."

"That's exactly the idea," Ben said. "In marathon training especially, your speed workouts shouldn't be superhard. It's important to keep that stimulus in the overall training mix, but just touch on it. Save your pain tolerance for the more marathon-specific workouts."

"Say, what time do you have?" I asked, suddenly remembering something. Ben checked his phone.

"Nine-fifty."

"Shit! I have a massage with Monica Coplea at Hypo2 at ten. Should I haul ass over there and skip the cool-down or do the cool-down and reschedule?"

Most professional runners get massages at least once a week, and most NAZ Elite members get them at Hypo2, where team membership entitles them to two free sessions per month and a discount on any additional bodywork. At home, I get massages only when I'm desperate, but I'm here to do what the pros do, and who can say no to free massages?

"Get out of here," Ben said.

Twelve minutes later, I was face down on a padded table wearing only my sweaty running shorts, dim lighting and gentle music fostering false expectations for the hour ahead, a lulling effect that was further augmented by Monica's soft-spoken self-presentation.

"Are there any problem areas you'd like me to focus on?" she asked.

"At this point in my life I'm pretty much held together by duct tape and coat hanger wire," I quipped. "But if I had to pick one spot, it would be my left Achilles. It's bothered me on and off for years, and today's workout seems to have aggravated it."

Monica's fingers worked with surgical precision to find and expose the places where pain lurked beneath my skin—knots and tight spots and inflamed areas that exploded with breath-halting discomfort when properly agitated. Pronouncing my calves "tight," Monica set about loosening them up with her thumbs, pressing and sliding like a miser trying to squeeze the last bit of toothpaste from the tube. More than once, in response to a groan or a burst of inappropriate laughter from me, Monica asked if the pressure was too much, and though it was indeed too much, I said it wasn't, wanting to measure up to the real pros in pain tolerance if nothing else.

85 Days to Chicago

Eight minutes past eleven o'clock this morning I poked my head out the front door of Matt's house, wondering where the hell Sarah Cotton was. Just then, Sarah's Jeep Wrangler came rumbling down Pullman Drive, ripped a savage right turn onto Amethyst Road, and stopped with a lurch in the driveway, where Matt doesn't like his guests' guests to park.

Sarah is a twenty-three-year-old videographer the team has hired to create an online series documenting the team's fall marathon buildup. A couple of days ago, Coach Ben allowed me to sit in on a planning meeting at his house with Sarah and the seven paid members of NAZ Elite running fall marathons. The hourlong discussion around the Rosario family dining room table was spirited and at times contentious, covering such topics as what to call the series, how to incorporate its sponsor, Roll Recovery, without shilling, how much "running porn" (workout footage) to include, and whether it was a good idea or a bad idea to portray the negative aspects of the pro running lifestyle.

"I think we should be really honest," Steph said. "Let's face it: There are parts of this job we all hate. Some days the last thing we want to do is run. If we're open about both the good and the bad, people will relate to us better."

"I'm not so sure about that," Matt countered. "I've seen other elites get trolled on Twitter for seeming ungrateful. 'Oh, poor you! Free shoes and an afternoon nap every day. What a terrible life!'"

"We're never going to please the haters," Faubs interjected. "Why should we censor ourselves for their sake?"

"These are all valid points," Coach Ben refereed. "To me, the important thing is authenticity. Just be yourselves. Steph, if you want to keep it real, don't hold back. Matt, if you're more comfortable focusing on the positives, that's fine too."

The meeting ended on a note of consensus, everyone agreeing that a good first step would be for Sarah to sit down with each athlete for an initial on-camera interview. Now it was my turn.

"Wow, nice house!" Sarah said as I showed her in.

It is a nice house: 2,750 square feet, dual master suites, hardwood floors, vaulted ceilings. Few professional runners can afford such a crib—nor could Matt himself, for that matter, before his breakthrough 1:01:47 half marathon three years ago. Matt's prior residence was a rented room in a sort of runners' flophouse owned by Alicia Vargo, widow of Ryan Shay, who died of a massive heart attack at age twenty-six while competing in the 2007 Olympic trials marathon. Matt did little more than sleep there, though, his waking hours dominated by long shifts as a grocery store clerk bookended by solitary runs undertaken in a single-minded quest to make it as a professional runner, a quest that had lured him to Flagstaff sight-unseen in the summer of 2012 with "no coach, no training partners, and no financial support," as he put it in one interview.

The odds were long. Overshadowed at Maryland's Broadneck High School by teammate and future world and Olympic champion Matthew Centrowitz, Matt did his collegiate running at unheralded University of

Richmond, where his best performance was an eighteenth-place finish in the 2011 NCAA championships 10,000 meters. Now he's the one renting out rooms.

I led Sarah upstairs to the grandest of these rooms and showed her the cozy little seating area where Nataki and I make a habit of passing our evenings, Nataki watching YouTube videos while I update the blog I'm keeping on my fake pro runner experience, compression boots squeezing my tired legs. Pronouncing the lighting perfect and the background suitable, Sarah indicated where I should sit and positioned herself at an appropriate distance.

"First of all," she said from behind the camera, "tell me about your background in running. How long have you been a runner?"

"The first mile I ever ran was the last mile of the 1983 Boston Marathon," I said. "My father is also a writer, and at the time he was working on a novel about a runner dying of ALS. For research purposes he ran Boston as a bandit, and my two brothers and I crossed the finish line with him. That was a pretty cool experience for an eleven-year-old kid, and when we got back home, I started running six miles every other day. At first it was mainly just a way to condition myself for soccer, but I figured out pretty quickly that I was a lot better at running, so I quit soccer and ran cross country and track in high school, where I was the top guy on a couple of state champion teams."

"Which state?" Sarah asked.

"New Hampshire," I confessed. "Not exactly a breeding ground for Olympians. And, believe me, I had no illusions. I knew I wasn't gifted enough to run professionally, but I still dreamed of finding out how good I could be. But then, for some reason, I just stopped improving. In hindsight, I think it had to do with the revolving door of mediocre coaches we had. In any case, I was too young and immature to figure it out on my own and, long story short, I got frustrated and quit. It's probably the worst decision I've ever made."

I stole a sideward glance at Nataki, who sat watching from the bed. She had never heard me say what I'd just said to this near stranger, and

I vaguely feared a negative reaction, but her face showed only neutral interest.

"I thought I would never run again," I resumed. "But when I moved to California after college, I stumbled into a job as a writer for a triathlon magazine, and the old spark was reignited. I've been getting after it ever since."

"So, you're not a professional runner yourself," Sarah said, "but you're here in Flagstaff training with a professional running team for the Chicago Marathon. How did that come about?"

"When I got back into running, I wanted to realize the potential I'd left unfulfilled when I gave it up," I said. "But I'm very injury-prone, and I just couldn't stay healthy long enough to achieve my goals. Then, before I knew it, I was forty years old, forty-one, forty-two, and I had to accept that I'd missed my chance."

The specific moment I had in mind occurred at the age of forty-three years, four months, and twenty-two days, to be precise. I had recently overcome yet another injury and worked myself back into fairly decent shape, and I decided to test my fitness in a half marathon. My goal was modest and, I thought, realistic. Having averaged 5:35 per mile in my best half marathon six years earlier, I was content to run fifteen seconds slower in this one. But I couldn't do it. After ten miles I felt as though I were wading through waist-deep molasses, and a mile later I dropped out, utterly defeated. I realized then, with crushing certainty, that my best days as a runner were past, and worse, that my best days weren't very good. Despite all I'd invested in the pursuit of my potential, it just hadn't happened, and I grieved the loss. They say athletes die twice, and, well, I get it.

"Last year," I told Sarah, "I read *Paper Lion*, a book George Plimpton wrote in the 1960s. Plimpton was not an athlete; he was just this gangly literary guy with a phony patrician accent, but he loved sports and he had moxie and he convinced the Detroit Lions football team to let him participate in their summer training camp as a backup quarterback, and his book recounts the experience. The whole time I was reading it, I kept imagining myself trying the same experiment in running."

"And so . . ." Sarah prompted.

"The thing is," I said, "there are so many runners out there who are just like me—men and women and boys and girls who wonder how good they could be if they took it all the way. But the reality is that only a handful of super-talented youngsters get the opportunity to find out—the ones who win the genetic lottery at conception and get an early start in the sport and perform well in college and earn shoe contracts that allow them to pursue a running-centered lifestyle supported by all of the resources they need to fully honor their gift. Plimpton's book got me thinking: *What difference might it have made for me as a not-super-talented runner to have had such an opportunity?* And then I thought, *Heck, what difference might it make for me even now?* Next thing I know, I'm emailing Ben Rosario, whom I knew a bit from my work as a writer, and asking him if he's ever read *Paper Lion.* He got it instantly, and now here I am. I might have missed my chance to become the best runner I could be, but I can still experience what it's like to try."

"You've been here for a week," Sarah said. "How has it been so far?"

"I love the simplicity of this way of living," I said. "My days revolve around running. Everything I do from the time I wake up to the time I go to bed has the clear and singular objective of making me a better runner. There's something almost spiritual about the clean, stripped-down Spartanism of it."

"And you plan to write about this?" Sarah asked.

"I came here not only to have an experience but to share it," I said. "I'd be lying if I told you I didn't hope that maybe my best days as a runner are not behind me after all. But whether that's true or not, I've come to believe that talent shouldn't determine how far a person goes with their running. Passion should. My hope is that, if this whole fake pro runner thing goes well, I can inspire other runners to do something similar to what I'm doing here."

What I did not tell Sarah is that, for me, "goes well" has a precise, numerical definition: a sub-2:40 marathon in Chicago.

83 Days to Chicago

Arizona Snowbowl (or just Snowbowl, as locals call it) is a ski resort perched high atop the San Francisco Peaks north of Flagstaff. In the summer, when the snow melts, runners and hikers take over its network of trails, and though it's a bit out of the way for most members of NAZ Elite, Coach Ben likes to take the team up the mountain at least once per season for an easy run, and he did so today. We met at Aspen Corner, a trailhead near the summit, Nataki and I tailing Coach Ben there from his house to ensure we didn't get lost (as new visitors have been known to do). The first person I greeted upon debouching from the Fun Mobile was Scott Smith, and it was to him that I put the question I'd been pondering during our long ascent.

"What's the elevation here?"

"Nine thousand feet," Scott said.

"Holy shit! What's the rationale for running this high up?"

"It's beautiful."

"I meant the physiological rationale."

Scott gave me a queer look, as though I'd asked him for the nutritive value of cheesecake.

"There is none," he said. "It's just beautiful."

After the usual preliminaries, we filed into the woods, the trail quickly narrowing to singletrack, squeezing the group of eleven into a pace-ordered conga line. I took my usual position at the back with Coach Ben, who played tour guide, waxing poetic about our surroundings as we picked our way through a grove of aspen trees, emerging after a couple of miles into a vast glen at the far end of which lay a majestic view of the forest below.

"You should see what it looks like here in September," he said. "When the aspen leaves turn, all of this becomes a golden yellow. You'd swear you're running through a painting."

I dared not risk a lingering look at the splendor before me, wary of stubbing a toe on a rock and face-planting, but I took in as much as I could in furtive glances. Just past four miles, we bumped into Steph and Ben Bruce, Amy, and Anne Marie Blaney, a visiting runner from Central Florida University, who had come to a dead stop on a particularly tricky section of the trail.

"What's going on?" Coach Ben asked.

"There was a fall," Ben Bruce said.

Evidently Amy had done just what I'd feared doing myself: tripped over a stone and gone down hard. Her right shoulder was covered in grit and she had a small gash on her left shin. Otherwise unhurt, she brushed herself off and resumed running.

Farther along, Coach Ben and I found the same group halted again, this time in the middle of a broad meadow carpeted in dry grasses bending in a warm breeze.

"Not again!" I said. "Who was it this time?"

"No one," Steph said. "We're admiring the view."

Coach Ben and I turned in the direction the others were facing. I half expected to hear "The Sound of Music" as I took in the pristine alpine landscape that cascaded away from our feet toward an unreachable horizon. Amid the awed silence I was struck by the thought that my companions were working right now, clocked in at the office, or their version thereof.

When we got moving again, Amy, perhaps now feeling the bruises she'd acquired, slid back and ran alongside me.

"What's the name of that muscle again?" I asked, referring to the spot of her pelvic injury.

"Obturator internus," she said.

"How's it feeling today?" I asked.

"About the same. I've been researching it. I learned it's a common problem area in people who have previously had osteitis pubis, which I have. I now know more than I ever wanted to about pelvic anatomy." Amy laughed ruefully. "But I do feel better knowing than not knowing."

"I can relate," I said. "I've had a few mystery injuries over the years, and it's almost like the mystery part is worse than the injury part."

No sooner had I spoken these words than I regretted them. Who was I to compare my situation to Amy's? Like all professional sports, running is a what-have-you-done-for-me-lately business. Amy's last big win came more than a year and a half ago, and she's been injury-plagued ever since. Coach Ben seems to have genuine affection for every member of the team, but he can only afford to devote resources to a hobbled athlete who isn't racing—and racing well—for so long, and Amy is very much aware of this reality. I know *nothing* of that sort of pressure.

"It's frustrating, though, you know?" Amy said, seeming not to notice the foot in my mouth. "Sometimes I wish I could just . . . run."

The run concluded with a tough climb back to the trailhead. Amy's breathing became audible, and I moved ahead of her. Anne Marie grunted a couple of times and Steph muttered some complaint I didn't quite catch. Meanwhile, I felt terrific, and at the top of the hill I found myself ahead of everyone except Ben Bruce.

After a quick round of high fives, I went to check on Nataki and Queenie, meditating on my earlier exchange with Scott Smith as I walked. Perhaps, I thought, a person doesn't have to sacrifice one or the other—beauty or practical benefit—when choosing a place to run. Perhaps the more beautiful your environment is, the happier you are, and the happier you are, the better your body feels, and the better your body feels, the better you run.

82 Days to Chicago

Once a week, often but not always on a Tuesday, the team gathers for an afternoon session of drills, strides, and "plyos" (short for *plyometrics*, or jumping exercises). Coach Ben held me out of last week's session, wanting to avoid throwing too much at me all at once, but today I got to participate. Sort of.

Sunday's team email instructed the group to meet at NAU Fields, which, I assumed, referred to athletic fields on the campus of Northern Arizona University. The campus is large, though, and I hadn't yet set foot on it, so this morning I collared Matt Llano in (where else?) the kitchen, where he was elbow-deep in a mixing bowl, baking superhero muffins from his friend and fellow professional runner Shalane Flanagan's cookbook, *Run Fast, Eat Slow*, and asked him how to get there. Matt set down the whisk and described the way in careful detail, concluding with four words you never want to hear when someone is giving you directions: "You can't miss it."

Well, I missed it, parking at the first set of athletic fields I came to on the NAU campus and failing to locate the correct set until the real pros were finishing up.

"You just wanted individualized attention, didn't you?" Coach Ben called out as I sprinted toward him from the gate, cheeks aflame.

"Actually, I would have preferred *not* to be the center of attention," I answered.

Lounging together at the edge of the field were Ben's wife, Jen; their five-year-old daughter, Addison; and interns Ian and Veronica. Presumably, they'd all had stuff to do while the real pros were present, but now they had the look of a panel of figure skating judges.

With an abrupt hand clap Ben signaled that it was time to get serious.

"So," he began. "Drills, strides, and plyos: What are they for? There are three main things we try to accomplish with them. The first is to increase range of motion, especially at the hips. Most runners have tight hips, which can really mess up their stride, and you'll see that some of the drills we do are designed to open up the hips. The second objective is to reduce ground contact time. The quicker you can get your feet off the ground when you run, the better. Marathon training has a tendency to do the opposite, so we do certain drills and plyos to counteract that. And, finally, we like to do drills that isolate and strengthen certain phases of the stride, particularly the pawback, when you're retracting your leg just before footstrike. That also helps with ground contact time."

"You would have made a great teacher," I interjected.

Ben carried on as though he hadn't heard me. "Now, I will admit that the old-school part of me wonders if this shit actually works or if it's just a big waste of time," he said. "But there are two reasons I think it does work."

The first reason, he explained, was personal experience. Ben did not incorporate drills, strides, and plyos into his own training until his late twenties, after he'd left the Michigan-based Hansons-Brooks team, moved back to his native St. Louis, and shifted his focus from the marathon to the mile. Having run no faster than 4:19 at the shorter distance at Division II Truman State University, he subsequently lowered his time to 4:03. The second reason had to do with what Ben had observed in the runners he coaches.

"Most runners, when they first start doing this stuff, are terrible at it," he said. "But as the weeks go by, they get better and better. Admittedly, drills and strides aren't the same thing as running, but they are related to it. The bottom line is that doing this stuff turns runners into better athletes, and my thinking is, How can that be a bad thing?"

If Ben's intent in telling me that even most elite runners make fools of themselves the first time they do what I was about to do was to assuage my fear of doing the same, he failed miserably. Despite my apprehension, I got off to a decent start, managing to skip forward while making circles with my arms and to shuffle sideways while crossing and spreading my arms without major incident.

Things took a decided turn for the worse, however, when we moved on to A skips, which entail hopping forward on one foot while driving the opposite knee upward. I'd completed just four or five of these when I caught Ben chuckling in the periphery of my vision.

"What?" I asked, stopping.

"Your arms are all wrong. Concentrate on moving them normally, like you do when you're running. You're going like *this*."

Ben proceeded to crank his arms back and forth in such an absurdly exaggerated manner that I had to fight back an urge to protest. I couldn't possibly have looked *that* ridiculous . . . could I?

Moving on, Ben showed me B skips, which are the same as A skips except the driving leg is snapped to full extension on the way to the ground. I gave them a go and was just getting the hang of them (I thought) when Ben laughed again. I glared at him: *Now what?*

"Try going in a straight line," he said.

Next up was a modified backward running drill that required me to reach behind my reversing body with a fully straightened leg, a silly-looking drill even if you're doing it perfectly, which, apparently, I wasn't.

"Is your left Achilles bothering you?" Ben asked.

I told him it was.

"Thought so. You're not getting nearly as much extension on that side."

Relief came when we transitioned from drills to strides. After all, strides are nothing more than running: short, relaxed sprints done at a little less than full speed.

"This is the one time I want you to really think about your form," Ben said before sending me off. "Pretend that *Runner's World* is here doing a photo shoot and you want to put on a show for the camera."

The grass athletic field we were standing on was in fact a regulation football field, complete with hash marks. My task was to run from one end zone to the other—100 yards. No problem. On Ben's command I launched, trying to channel my inner Carl Lewis (High knees! Run tall!), but almost immediately I felt as though I were dragging an invisible parachute. Only then did it occur to me that I hadn't run an honest sprint in years, a concession to my body's sundry trouble spots. Before I'd even reached midfield I was already losing speed, and as I crossed the far end zone, stooped under the weight of an invisible piano, I thanked God that a *Runner's World* photographer was not actually present to memorialize my disgrace.

After a short rest I charged back toward Ben, determined to do better. At the forty-yard line my body began to shudder like a shoddily built Russian spacecraft making a doomed reentry to earth's atmosphere. Conscious of my audience, I focused again on trying to run like Carl Lewis, but when I got close enough to read faces I saw undisguised pity written on each of them, and I wanted to disappear.

"Your form was eroding a bit near the end," Ben observed amusedly as I caught my breath. "Try resting a little longer before the next one."

Extra rest didn't help, and the last labored steps of my final rep elicited another smiling headshake from Ben.

"You were doing that thing where your left arm flares out like this," he said, imitating an eccentricity of my running form that I don't notice except when I see it in photos and videos. "Nothing you can do about it."

I followed Ben's eyes as he gazed over at the speed ladder and mini hurdles the real pros had used earlier for the plyometric portion of the session.

"Let's save the toys for another time," he said. "After you've mastered the basics."

Ian and Veronica scrambled to gather up the training implements I'd been judged too incompetent to mess with, and we all made our way toward the parking lot.

"Well, that was humbling," I said.

"You did fine," Ben assured me. "Like I told you, everyone struggles at first. You'll get better, and as you do, your running will benefit. I've seen it happen many times."

I wanted very much to believe him.

81 Days to Chicago

We were on our mats again—Brauny, Scott Smith, Faubs, and I—discussing the workout we were about to do at a place called Kiltie Loop, another in Coach Ben's collection of good places for fast running, and I was confused.

"Why the mishmash?" I asked my teammates. "To me it looks like two different workouts squished together."

At home, my workouts always focus on a single intensity—5K pace, marathon pace, whatever. This one had two distinct parts: a set of one-kilometer repeats at critical velocity (the highest speed a runner can sustain for about thirty minutes) followed by 200-meter repeats at one-mile race effort. As usual, I'd been given a scaled-down version of the pros' agenda: eight times 1K in 3:42 plus six times 200 meters in 37 seconds for me, ten times 1K in 3:02 plus eight times 200 meters in 30 seconds for them.

It was Coach Ben who answered my question, having just then returned from a cone-placing mission.

"Well, as I'm sure you'd agree," he began, adopting his teaching voice, "a handful of 200s isn't much of a workout. And yet it's plenty of speed work if you're eleven or twelve weeks out from a marathon. At the same time, it would be kind of a waste to set aside a whole day for it. So, why not combine the 200s with something that's more specific to the marathon?"

"How about the order?" I asked. "Why do the faster stuff last?"

"Think about it," Ben said. "When, if ever, are you going to sprint in a marathon? That's right: at the very end, on very tired legs. I want my athletes to know what that feels like before it really matters!"

Eric "Big Dog" Fernandez had again been enlisted to serve as my pacer, and again he blew in late, after I'd warmed up with two laps around the wooded neighborhood and just in time for the fun stuff. He looked like he'd gained five pounds of mostly muscle since the last time I saw him, and I told him so.

"Really?" he said, radiant. "I hope you're serious."

Despite the weight gain, and despite his having run exactly zero miles since the last time I saw him, Eric had no trouble whatsoever in carrying out his duties, and as I ran along in his long shadow I was seized by a low-grade jealousy, a must-be-nice envy of this carefree man-boy's ability to joke his way through an interval set that ninety-five out of a hundred people couldn't complete with any amount of training, when all he'd done to prepare was pump iron and overeat intentionally. Yet the target pace Coach Ben had given me felt pretty darn easy for me as well, and I made a point of letting him know it during a short break between parts one and two of the workout.

"Easy doesn't necessarily mean *too* easy," Ben cautioned, catching the note of complaint in my voice. "Feeling good today is what earns you faster paces next time."

Part two was even easier in principle but worried me more, not because I suck at speed work but because I was barely able to get out of bed this morning, my ailing left Achilles tendon having hardened like drying cement overnight. If shuffling to the toilet at a nonagenarian's pace was painful, I wondered, how the hell was I going to survive one 200-meter semisprint, let alone six of them? Half expecting the aggrieved tendon to pop like an overtightened guitar string at any moment, I was thankful that it merely frayed a little more with each repetition and left me limping slightly after the last of them. My last remaining challenge was to walk back to the Fun Mobile without anyone noticing the hitch in my giddyup.

"Are you limping?" Faubs asked as I passed.

So much for that.

"No," I said reflexively. "Well, yes. I've got an Achilles thing that has bothered me on and off for years. I expected it to act up here at some point—I was just kind of hoping it wouldn't be this soon."

"Maybe you should pop down to Phoenix and see John Ball. Craig had really bad Achilles problems. Saw John twice. No more problems."

"I've heard he's a piece of work."

John Ball's name has come up frequently in my short time here. A chiropractor by training, he functions as a full-service physical therapist to a clientele of mainly world-class athletes who flock from all over the country for consultations that cost up to 400 bucks a pop. Stories abound. Ben Bruce described him to me the other day as "the House M.D. of chiropractors," by which, I gathered, he meant an arrogant savant of the healing arts who suffers no fools and plays by his own rules. Others present—all of them devoted patients—tossed out the adjectives "condescending," "mean," and "sadistic." Matt sees him twice a month for his surgically repaired hips. At his latest appointment, he told me, John greeted him with the words, "You need to eat a sandwich." Steph says that if you make the mistake of asking John what caused a particular injury, expecting one of those anatomical just-so stories ("Actually, your toe pain is the result of a muscle imbalance in your neck") that others in John's line of work love to tell, he will look you in the eye and say witheringly, "Running."

"John Ball is . . . an experience," Faubs said. "The first time I saw him, he had his thumb on my grundle within five minutes. His pinkie was two centimeters away from my ball sac. It hurt like a motherfucker."
"Say no more," I said. "I'll take the next available appointment."

79 Days to Chicago

Before Nataki and I left California, I promised her I'd take her out to dinner every Friday throughout our stay in Flagstaff—an undisguised bribe intended to forestall any potential objections she might have to my being 100 percent running-focused the rest of the time. We initiated the ritual last week at Criollo, a self-described "Latin kitchen" located on trendy South San Francisco Street in the heart of downtown, where the menu was hit-or-miss, Nataki enjoying her bison meatloaf somewhat less than I did my paella special.

"I blame myself," I said to her between bites of a churro that we ordered for sharing but I ate all but one bite of.

My mistake had been to seek restaurant recommendations from my new teammates, who for reasons of age (Craig, Futsum) or income (pretty much everyone except Matt and Kellyn) or lifestyle (Steph and Ben Bruce, with their two small boys) seldom dine out, except at paper-napkin joints like Pizzicletta and Diablo Burger. I promised Nataki I would do better this week by conducting my own, independent research, an effort that began and ended yesterday when I saw a flyer taped to a wall at Hypo2 that advertised a place called Proper Meats. *With a name like that,* I thought . . .

Another mistake. The pork barbecue sandwich I ate was delicious. That wasn't the problem. The problem was that *it was a pork barbecue sandwich* (with a side of french fries, no less), and I bathed in guilt as I devoured it, knowing Matt Llano would never grub on such garbage, except maybe after a race. Overall, I've been doing a pretty good job of emulating my host's clean, balanced, and inclusive diet. Prior to tonight's lapse, for example, I breakfasted on low-sugar whole-grain granola with fresh strawberries and organic whole milk and lunched on broiled salmon with brown rice and a broccoli salad. But this only made the lapse itself seem all the more inexcusable. Adding insult to injury, Proper Meats was not the white tablecloth establishment of my visions but a casual sandwich and deli shop, and Nataki and I arrived absurdly overdressed.

"I don't know what the hell I was thinking," I lamented, reaching across a grease-splattered Formica tabletop to snatch a cold burnt potato crumb from Nataki's plate.

When we got back to the house it was still fairly early, and Matt was busy preparing his own evening meal, one of his trademark bowls of kale and quinoa plus whatever healthy ingredients happened to be in the refrigerator. My shame redoubled.

"Are you going out later?" I asked.

"Not tonight," he said. "Dinner, Epsom salt bath, bed. That's my plan."

My own plan had been similar (minus the dinner part, which couldn't be undone), but something vaguely sad in the sound of Matt's words compelled us to linger, and before long the three of us were engrossed in a frank conversation about our host's social life, or lack thereof. Asked by Nataki if she and I were witnessing a typical Friday night in the life of Matt Llano, he confessed that when he has a major running goal in front of him—which is pretty much always—he tends to get tunnel vision, jettisoning any and all activities that do not contribute directly to the mission at hand.

"Ben and I actually had a long talk about it last year," he said. "He told me I needed to get out more and do some stuff just for the fun of it. That's when I started doing game night at the Brauns."

Last night Matt baked a batch of gluten-free macaroons (Aaron's wife, Annika, has an intolerance) and spent the evening at the couple's house playing Scrabble, a routine that he repeats two or three times a month.

"Has it helped?" I asked.

"To be honest, I don't mind being a hermit when there's a big race ahead. I kind of like it. At the same time, I think Ben is right, and it is good for me to loosen up a bit. Yesterday I didn't get home until after ten, which is late for me, and it wasn't the end of the world."

Another question popped into my head. I hesitated, unsure of its propriety, then went ahead and asked it.

"Are you dating anyone currently?"

"I am not," Matt said, sounding not at all put out. "The dating scene in Flagstaff is pretty small, and the gay dating scene is *really* small. I have a great life, don't get me wrong. I feel fortunate in so many ways. But there's a giant hole in the middle of it."

Matt was six or seven years old when he began to understand that he was different from other boys. He liked to play with dolls, most of his friends were girls, and he had "a flair for theatrics," as he put it in a recent personal essay published online. As he got older, he felt compelled to hide certain parts of himself, fearful that expressing his full identity would expose him to judgment and ridicule. At the same time, he felt driven to prove—at least to himself, if not to anyone else—that he wasn't weaker or less worthy than others just because he was attracted to his own sex. In high school, Matt earned straight As, was elected president of the National Honor Society, excelled in sports, and was voted "Most Likely to Succeed." In college, he was a triple major and an All-American runner, graduating with a 3.95 grade point average.

In 2013, Matt became the first gay professional runner ever to come out publicly. Fearing hostility, he was instead applauded. Yet even today he is fueled by a burning need to prove his mettle and to challenge stereotypes of gay men. The irony, which is not lost on him, is that this single-minded ambition is perhaps his greatest obstacle to finding lasting love.

"Running comes first for me, and it will continue to come first for the foreseeable future," he told us. "It's not easy to find someone who's okay with that."

Hearing this, Nataki (bless her heart) went straight into matchmaking mode. She mentioned our friend Cory, a successful psychologist, passionate amateur runner, and all-around great guy who was raised in Kenya and emigrated to the U.S. when he was seventeen. I gently reminded Nataki that Cory is happily married to our friend Wade. "And don't even mention Antwan!" I added. Antwan was Nataki's BFF when she and I started dating back in the late 1990s, but he's currently in prison.

As Nataki and I made our way upstairs a few minutes later, I wondered—not for the first time—if I might not be a better runner today if I'd had a more challenging youth.

76 Days to Chicago

I burst through the front door of Hypo2 at a trot, hustled through the building's now-familiar network of halls to AJ's office, and barged in without knocking, all apologies for my minor tardiness (the consequence of a meet-and-greet between NAZ Elite and a visiting high school cross country team that ran long), only to find AJ examining the knee of another patient, a woman in her fifties with the legs of a serious runner.

"Oh, sorry!" I said, coloring.

"I'll be just a few minutes," AJ said in the same placid tone of voice in which he says everything. (It's impossible to imagine the man yelling.) "There's some paperwork in the waiting area that I need you to fill out."

Fifteen minutes later I was back inside, slouching on a treatment table while AJ peppered me with questions about the Achilles tendon injury that had brought me to him. It started eight years ago, I explained, and has never fully healed, impervious to treatments ranging from active release to the Graston Technique. Only by modifying my natural running style to more of a Groucho Marx shuffle, which I retain to this day, was I able to return to running, and though there are times when it barely grumbles, the injury tends to flare up when I add faster running to my training, as I've done in recent weeks.

"I recommend that we treat it with cold laser and shockwave," AJ pronounced. "Those modalities will get in there much deeper than anything else you've tried. But first let's do some testing."

I was invited to take off my shoes and socks, stand on one foot, and swing the unsupported leg from side to side in front of my body, then back and forth like an old-school placekicker. I began on the left foot and finished on the right, AJ studying my lower extremities intently as I struggled to keep my balance.

"Do you see how you tend to roll onto the outside of your left foot but not your right?" he said. "There's obviously an asymmetry there. Now I want you to do the same thing but concentrate on pulling your big toe toward your heel while you swing the other leg . . . Good, just like that. Does it make a difference?"

It did. I felt my foot actively gripping the floor, like a toilet plunger suctioned to hardwood, whereas previously my body had felt more like a precariously tall stack of dishes.

AJ now asked me to stand on both feet and slowly bend both knees as though I were dropping my rear end onto a bench. I did this three or four times before AJ rendered his verdict.

"Do you see how your left arch is collapsing but not your right?" he asked.

I did. AJ explained that my foot itself was not to blame. More likely, he said, the source of the instability lay higher up.

Finally, I was instructed to lift my big toe and bend my knee while keeping the heel of the foot in contact with the floor, right side then left side.

"Do you see how you're able to get your right knee in front of your toes, but not your left?"

"Yes, dammit!" I said. "It seems I've failed every test. But how do we fix it? What exercises can you give me?"

"The tests *are* the exercises. Do them every day."

Treatment time. AJ ushered me over to a padded table and asked me to lie face down. Moments later an ear-splitting static-electric sound filled the room—the shockwave machine.

"It's going to feel like I'm tapping you with a small hammer," AJ said. "I want you to let me know when the pain level reaches two on a one-to-ten scale."

"How does this thing work?" I shouted.

"It stimulates angiogenesis," AJ said, setting to work, "which is a fancy way of saying it promotes the formation of new blood vessels. New blood vessels mean more blood flow. More blood flow means faster healing."

"Two!" I yelled.

We went through a similar process with the laser. AJ warned me there would be a heating sensation and told me to let him know when the warmth became painful. As he moved the beam in small circles against my skin, I asked him how the thing worked and was told something about cell membranes and the electron transport chain and mitochondria that went in one ear and out the other.

After ten minutes the machine beeped and shut itself off. The session then turned painfully low-tech, AJ digging his thumbs deeply into different points of my Achilles while using his thigh to flex my ankle. When he hit just the right spot, I gripped the edges of the table reflexively with clawed fingers. Speech was not an option in these moments, but on regaining control of my tongue I requested another explanation and learned that in some cases of Achilles pain, the real problem is adhesion of the plantaris muscle to the Achilles, which can cause repetitive friction during running. Because I felt pain *only* when running, AJ speculated, this rubbing action might be at least partly to blame.

My entire body felt like jelly as I dressed to leave.

"When can we do this again?" I joked.

"How about later this week?" AJ said, not joking.

I cocked an eyebrow.

"You're here to do what the pros do, right? So let's deal with this thing as if your job depends on it."

75 Days to Chicago

It's the trails, mainly, that make Flagstaff a runner's paradise, but the city's most famous running venue is paved. Lake Mary Road is known around the world to geeks like me as the proving ground for Flagstaff runners, the sunbaked blacktop measuring stick upon which legendary athletes including Ryan Hall and Paula Radcliffe have honed their bodies and minds for feats of greatness. Anchored in central Flagstaff, the aspen-lined two-lane highway charts an undulant, southerly course that extends far beyond the last of the distance markers that appear at quarter-mile intervals on its west shoulder, the work of Ben and Jen Rosario, who stenciled them shortly after they moved to Flagstaff from St. Louis in the fall of 2013 and ceremoniously repainted every spring.

I got my first taste of Lake Mary Road last weekend, and it tasted good. Coach Ben gave me a sixteen mile cutdown long run ending with a 6:20 mile that I ran in 5.53, coasting. Perhaps this was simply because the experiment is working, or because Ben Bruce, slowed by an abdominal strain, volunteered to pace me. But my hunch is that there's something about Lake Mary Road that suits the way I most like to run, which is in a trancelike groove where the suffering bubbles up slowly, as water comes to a boil at 7,000 feet.

Whatever the case, I was delighted to be called back to Lake Mary Road today, this time for a session of mile repeats followed by 200-meter sprints. The team met in a dirt parking area near Mile 1.5, in a hollow between two hills, our plan being to run the repeats back and forth from high point to high point

I was squatting with my hands braced against the Fun Mobile's rear bumper, a racquet ball squeezed in the crook of my left knee (a calf-loosening trick I learned from Monica Coplea during my last massage), when a bright-yellow Kia Soul pulled in and parked directly opposite. The driver's door opened and out popped the child-size figure of Rochelle

Kanuho, back from her two-week break. Despite having not seen most of her teammates since before the furlough, she greeted no one and stretched on her own, overdressed for the weather in a long-sleeve Hoka top.

Rochelle has an adventitious background for a professional runner. Born right here in Flagstaff, she was raised by a single mother, a high-school dropout who changed jobs as often as some people change their bedsheets, bouncing among low-wage gigs at laundromats, convenience stores, and the like. The pair were constantly on the move, from trailer home to motel room to relative's house and back to trailer home. Rochelle's stepfather, whose Navajo surname she carries, exited the picture when she was five, by which time she had accumulated seven half siblings. Erratic in mood and behavior, Rochelle's mom kept her indoors as much as possible and threw a fit whenever she made some normal kid mistake like spilling a drink. On the day she finished high school, Rochelle came home to find her few sad belongings piled outside a locked door. She never saw her mother again.

Running saved Rochelle from the fates that so often claim the children of chaos—but not right away. Having shown flashes of talent and a boundless enthusiasm for the sport as a teen, Rochelle got her first real break in life in the person of Diane Sorden, a track coach and guidance counselor at Coconino High School, who offered the displaced and abandoned young woman a place to stay during the summer before she matriculated at NAU. Lacking the credentials she needed to make the cross country team as a freshman, Rochelle spent the next year training alone at night on an unlit track, improving just enough to claim a roster spot the next fall. But she was still no match for her new teammates, and she finished dead last in every single workout—until her coach ordered a blood test, which revealed that Rochelle had severe anemia, the result of a lifetime of malnourishment. Within a week of starting iron supplementation, she had catapulted from last to first, and she remained the team's top performer for the next three years.

After graduating from NAU with a degree in parks and recreation, Rochelle was invited to join a post-collegiate running group based in

Colorado Springs. A professional runner in name only, she worked multiple jobs and lived rent-free in the home of her new coach. Despite these imperfect circumstances, Rochelle's running flourished, and her 5000-meter time dropped from 16:12 to 15:25 in a few short months. That's when Ben Rosario came calling.

In 2016, as a rookie member of NAZ Elite, Rochelle finished seventh in the Olympic Trials 5000 meters and recorded the year's seventh-fastest half-marathon time by an American woman (1:11:28). Fortune has been less kind to her this year, however, with minor injuries limiting her to just two races and a twentieth-place finish in the recent USA Track & Field Outdoor Championships 5000 meters.

Rochelle glanced my way a couple of times as we each loosened up some fifteen feet apart, but when I nodded at her, inviting verbal communication, she averted her eyes. After finishing with the lacrosse ball, I stood up, approached her directly, and gave her my right hand, searching my mind for an appropriate opener.

"What's your next race?" I ventured.

"I like running the Tufts 10K," Rochelle said, her dollish voice a perfect match for her waifish appearance. "That's in October. After that, I don't know. Maybe a half marathon?"

"How many times have you run Tufts?"

This would be her third time, she said.

"Are you the sort of person who always orders the same meal at restaurants?" I asked teasingly.

"Yes!" she laughed.

The session began with a three-mile jog on a forested dirt track branching off Lake Mary Road. I ran with James McKirdy, a Connecticut-based running coach who, with his girlfriend, Heather Szuba, recently took over the downstairs bedroom previously occupied by pro triathlete Jen Spieldenner at Matt's house.

"Are you sure you're up for this?" I asked him.

James had volunteered to pace me despite having a meniscus tear in his left knee that had severely restricted his recent training.

"Only one way to find out!" he said.

We completed our warm-up back on pavement, making our way to Mile 2—our starting point for the first mile repeat—by means of high knees, butt kicks, and A and B skips, a purely utilitarian measure that might have been mistaken for a reenactment of Monty Python's Ministry of Silly Walks skit by passing motorists. Ian and Veronica met us there, Coach Ben having deputized them to look after me while he took care of Matt, Faubs, and Brauny. I had promised Ben that, no matter how good I felt, I would run the odd-numbered reps (more up than down) in 6:35 and the easier even-numbered reps in 6:25—a touch faster than my current estimated marathon pace, adjusted for altitude. These times being vastly slower than those the real pros were assigned, James and I queued up ahead of them, shuffling over to a traffic cone positioned on the road's south shoulder and crouching like middle-distance racers at the start line.

Something about this familiar tableau must have triggered a Pavlovian response in James, who won back-to-back decathlon state titles in high school, because the moment I took my first step my putative pacer shot ahead of me like a panicked beachgoer fleeing a fifty-foot tidal wave. This move, in turn, flipped some atavistic switch in me, and I tore after him.

"What's your pace again?" James asked when I caught up.

"Six thirty-five," I said.

"Oh," James said sheepishly. "I thought it was *five* thirty-five."

Just beyond the half-mile cone, Matt, Faubs, and Brauny blew past us on their way to a 4:55 split.

"Feel free to join them if I'm holding you back," I grumbled at James.

Coach Ben and the interns awaited us at the finish, having driven there.

"Six twelve!" Veronica called out as we passed the finish cone.

Ben threw up his arms in the manner of a football coach protesting a bullshit holding penalty.

"That's my mulligan," I said, circling around. "I'll nail the next one, promise."

I did not nail the next one. Or the one after that.

The problem, I decided, was that the route's extreme topography made proper pacing much trickier than it would have been on a flat route. Also, my watch disagreed with the paint marks on the road, and though the latter were unquestionably more accurate, I am accustomed (like most amateurs) to relying on my watch. Furthermore, a 6:12 mile simply *felt* like a 6:35 mile to me, even at 7,000 feet.

Having somehow gotten stronger as the workout wore on, James towed me through a flagrantly disobedient 6:05 final mile. We then shambled down to the base of the U, where a pair of cones had been placed 200 meters apart, for the dreaded second part of the workout: the sprints. The shredding of my left Achilles tendon picked up right where it had left off at Kiltie Loop six days ago, but as before, the dream-killing rupture I feared most didn't happen, and the weary high five I offered James after sprint number eight expressed as much relief as it did esprit de corps. Now it was time to face the music.

"Don't get me wrong," Coach Ben said to me back at the parking area as we reviewed the workout, "I'm happy you're feeling strong. But I'm giving you these times for a reason. Just because you *can* run faster doesn't mean you *should*. I want to see you do better in the future. Why are you laughing?"

"Sorry," I said, still laughing. "I'm just having so much fun!"

74 Days to Chicago

"Very slow today, very slow."

Coach Ben spoke these words from the threshold of his home as Nataki and I waded toward him across the overgrown front yard. Yesterday I made the mistake of sharing a candid status report on my throbbing left Achilles on my blog, which Ben somehow found the time to read. I was now under orders to make today's eight-mile easy run extra easy to avoid further aggravating the injury.

Inside the house, we loitered around the dining room table (the same one where Sarah Cotton had presided over the fall marathon documentary kickoff meeting) while my teammates entered by ones and twos, none of them knocking, each taking his or her turn to sign a Northern Arizona Elite jersey that was to be presented later in the day to a booster who happens to be in town. When a quorum-making Aaron Braun added his signature, everyone poured back outside to run.

"How am I going to avoid getting lost if I'm alone behind everyone?" I asked Ben, sounding more whiney than I'd intended.

"I'll stay with you," Steph volunteered.

Rochelle, running for only the second time since her break, hung back also as Veronica trailed us on a mountain bike through Ben's neighborhood of smallish, mostly single-story houses to the nearest trailhead, which wasn't far away (because *no* house in Flagstaff stands far from the nearest trailhead).

"What's it like to be famous?" I asked Steph, apropos of nothing.

She laughed—not because I was joking but because I *wasn't* joking. Steph had become legitimately famous when she posted a photo of her stomach on Instagram shortly after she gave birth to her second child, Hudson. For the most part, Steph looks like your typical supremely fit elite runner, but the one part that doesn't is a small patch of wrinkly loose skin on her belly, a post-partum condition known medically as diastasis recti that will never go away. It's the kind of thing a lot of women in her position would have kept hidden, but Steph did the opposite, a choice that took more courage than most of us can appreciate, given the vicious online body shaming Steph (like so many female athletes) was subjected to even before her tummy got stretched out.

In 2014, for example, a pre-pregnancy picture of Steph was published on womensrunning.com alongside a blog post she'd written for the website. One reader thought fit to comment, "This picture is sick and you are destroying your body. [You are] not a role model for our women and young girls!" Yet Steph refused to be shamed, and ironically it was this very defiance that turned her into a role model for women and girls across America and beyond. Steph has nearly 13,000 Twitter followers, far more than any other member of NAZ Elite.

"Honestly, I don't mind it," she said. "I feel that connecting with other runners is part of my job, and it's also something I enjoy. I never expected to bond with women runners in the way I have, but I'm grateful for it and I want to see where it leads."

After four miles, Steph peeled off in search of extra distance, leaving me with Rochelle and Veronica. They'd been absorbed in a conversation of their own while I quizzed Steph about her celebrity, and I now tuned in, seeking an opening.

"You can just give them some food and leave them alone for a week," Rochelle was saying.

"Are you talking about cats?" I asked.

"Yes," Rochelle said.

"How many do you have?"

"None. But we had lots of them when I was growing up . . . or my sister did."

I knew enough about Rochelle's unconventional upbringing to refrain from asking how it was that her sister had cats and she did not.

"I had a cat when I met Nataki," I offered, "but she was deathly allergic to it, so eventually I had to choose between them."

"Oh, that's a tough one," Rochelle mused. "Cat or person. Hmmm . . ."

Not sure if she was kidding or not, I let this remark go and the conversation moved on, wandering across various topics and landing eventually on running.

"How is your body holding up so far?" Rochelle asked me as we made our final approach to Coach Ben's house.

"Funny you should ask," I said. "Right now my left Achilles is killing me."

"I can tell from your stride. You're compensating."

Rochelle meant that I was running asymmetrically, favoring my injured side. As much as I hated to do so, I shared her observation with Ben when he came outside to welcome our return.

"Let's have you take tomorrow off," he said. "Sometimes with these things that's all it takes. And on Friday we'll have you do an easy run instead of leg speed. How does that sound?"

"It sounds terrible," I sulked.

A single day off wasn't the end of the world, I knew, but I had less confidence than Ben did that one day would do the job. And then what? I've been in Flagstaff less than three weeks and already my body is falling apart. Even if forty-eight hours of rest does help, will I be able to survive another ten weeks of even harder training?

After lunch, still moping, I changed into a fresh set of workout clothes, intending to walk on Matt's treadmill, something I've been doing a few times a week to get my aerobic exercise volume up to pro level without subjecting my legs to more high impact than they can handle. While I laced my shoes, Nataki asked if I wanted her to keep me company in the garage, but I was so deep in my brooding that I didn't hear her, so she asked again.

"I don't know!" I snapped. "Whatever. You decide."

In the evening, *still* moping, I went back downstairs to grab a handful of cashews (the only evening snack I've been allowing myself) and found Matt with his head in the refrigerator, gathering items for another ninety-nine-ingredient dinner bowl. Next thing I knew, words were tumbling out of me, a full confession of the anguish I felt about my injury and the remorse I felt over lashing out at Nataki.

"I'm the same way," Matt said soothingly, embracing the father confessor role I'd thrust on him. "Anyone on the team will tell you I'm not always the most fun guy to be around when I can't run."

"I just want this so bad," I said, close to tears. "It's absurd. I'm not even a real pro. None of this matters."

"I don't think it's absurd," Matt said.

70 Days to Chicago

Two vehicles, neither belonging to anyone I knew, sat parked on the western edge of Woody Mountain Road—an unpaved, twenty-six-mile *dead end* that's part of the team's regular rotation of picturesque running venues—when I arrived there at ten minutes to seven this morning, portending a big turnout. Sure enough, over the next quarter of an hour at least a dozen more cars and trucks rolled in, a majority of them expelling runners I had never seen before.

"Who are all these people?" I asked Ben Bruce.

"Flagstaff Long Runs," he said. "Local running group. Coach Ben likes to have us run with them once in a while. You know, community spirit."

From the tone of these words, I sensed that Ben would have preferred to sleep another hour and run with the usual crew at the usual time.

Last to arrive, as usual, was Kellyn Taylor. Instead of pulling an exercise mat out of her truck and flopping around on the ground like the rest of us, she stood apart with her arms folded above an exposed midriff that looked as though it could stop a bullet, glaring not quite at us, all but tapping her foot in impatience. According to Coach Ben, Kellyn simply refuses to take part in the fancy pre- and post-run exercises that the vast majority of 21st-century professional runners judge indispensable. She scarcely has time for them, what with her firefighter training and her eight-year-old daughter, Kylyn, to look after, but Ben suspects she would eschew such frivolities even if she had all day for them.

An original member of NAZ Elite, Kellyn has earned a reputation within and beyond the team as a hard woman who believes that hard miles and a hard head are the keys to success in running, and that everything else is a distraction. A tweet she posted recently reads, "I don't think you have to be the most talented person to perform well . . . I just think you have to be the toughest." Anyone who knows her can share a few good stories of Kellyn being Kellyn. Ben himself likes to tell the one about the massage she got before the 2016 Olympic Trials Marathon in Los Angeles from a New Age dude who did energy work on the side. Kellyn is the type of person whose most devoted friends warn you about before you meet her for the first time, but this poor fellow wasn't warned, and he therefore made the mistake of holding his palms several inches away from Kellyn's body near the end of the session, closing his eyes, and asking, "Do you feel that?"

"No," she told him flatly.

One morning, Kellyn showed up at a team workout covered in nasty scrapes, having fallen during a solo trail run the day before. "You should see the mountain lion," she said before anyone could ask.

Coach Ben arrived with a carful of new shoes from Hoka. He was passing by with an armload of boxes containing footwear in Faubs's size when Kellyn stopped him with a question: "Are we going to run or what?" No "Good morning," not even a "Yo, Coach!" Just that.

Minutes later, Kellyn had her wish, our large group quickly dividing amoeba-like into two smaller ones, male pros and ambitious amateurs striding off the front, female pros and guys like me falling back. Had there been an even slower group, I would have fallen back even farther. The reason was Kellyn, who treats long runs like others do yard work: the sooner done, the better. After four miles, Kellyn abandoned any pretense of not being in charge and dragged us through splits of 7:01, 7:00, 6:56, 6:58, and 6:56. On a downhill section of Mile 6 I looked at my watch and saw that my current pace was 6:28 per mile.

"Don't tell Ben," I announced, "but I am now running at the same pace I averaged in my last marathon."

"Well, Coach," Steph said, deepening her voice, "the good news is that the girls are getting really fit. The bad news is that I ran with them."

Everyone laughed, but I laughed loudest, understanding team dynamics well enough to know that to become the butt of jokes is—up to a point, anyway—to be accepted.

Amy, still nursing her pelvis injury, turned around at six miles, Steph at eight. At nine miles, just after the NAZ Elite members among us grabbed water bottles off a table set up by Coach Ben (who was meeting us at three-mile intervals), Kellyn charged on alone and I stopped for a potty break with my only remaining companions, a pro runner named Sarah Crouch and a stranger named Bob Tusso.

"Raise your hand if you want to keep running six-forty miles on the way back," I called out from behind the aspen I'd ducked behind to pee.

No hands went up. Yet our pace stayed pretty hot through the second half of the run. Sarah swore she wasn't responsible, but I think she was. The handshake she gave me when we introduced ourselves left my fingers throbbing. Indeed, she reminds me of Kellyn somewhat. Bob, on the other hand, with his bushy beard and folksy, mellifluous voice, seemed more of a go-with-the-flow type of guy than a pace setter. I could picture him on backcountry skiing adventures or playing bass guitar in a blues rock band.

Sarah's workout (she is coached by Houston-based running savant Steve Magness) required her to execute a few short surges on the way back to our starting point. Left alone with Bob during these brief desertions, I showered him with get-to-know-you questions and learned that he's an uphill skiing fanatic and plays bass guitar in a blues rock band. One of Coach Ben's private clients, he's currently training for the New York City Marathon, where he hopes to knock a few minutes off his personal best of 2:45.

At sixteen miles I began to fantasize about lunch, an early indicator of fatigue. As though she'd read my mind, Sarah chose this moment to ask if I have a favorite post–long run indulgence.

"I was just starting to crave pizza," I confessed. "Not that I'll actually eat a slice anytime soon. I'm on the Matt Llano diet. What's yours?"

"Taco Bell," she said. "But only after races. Don't judge."

When we got back to our starting point Sarah plowed on, needing two more miles to round out her assigned twenty. Bob shrugged and went with her, while I stopped to brief Coach Ben on my experience, suppressing a perverse temptation to repeat Steph's good news/bad news line. No sooner had Ben moved on to catch up with the real pros than a younger guy who'd run with the fast group approached me.

"Are you the author?" he asked.

Such is the measure of my fame. *Hey, aren't you that guy?* I confirmed my name and got his: Alex Harrison. In the conversation that ensued, I learned that Alex lives and works in Moab, Utah, but comes here once or twice a month because he lacks good running partners there.

"What brings you to Flagstaff?" he asked.

I explained the whole fake pro runner thing.

"What's your goal for Chicago?"

"I don't know yet," I said automatically.

"Dude!" said Sarah Crouch, who'd returned just in time to overhear this exchange. "After what I saw from you today, I'll be shocked if you don't break two thirty-five."

"Oh, great," I said. "No pressure there."

"I'm running Chicago, too," Alex said.

"What's *your* goal?" I asked.

There was a lengthy silence, Alex appearing to be genuinely afraid to answer.

"Two thirty-five," he said eventually.

"Wonderful!" I raved. "Sarah here says I'm going to kick your ass!"

AUGUST

67 Days to Chicago

Ever since Coach Ben ordered me to take last Thursday off to rest my degenerating left Achilles and then held me out of the next day's leg speed workout, I've been counting the hours to today's tempo run, studying the coded description of the session on Final Surge (the website Ben uses to deliver training prescriptions) the way I once mooned over a certain remote control car in the 1980 Sears Wish Book. Fourteen miles on Lake Mary Road, including four two-mile tempo efforts at 6:25 per mile. I *needed* this run, mentally as much as physically, regarding it as symbolic of getting back on track toward Chicago.

At a dinner held last night at Pizzicletta in celebration of Matt's twenty-ninth birthday, I asked Coach Ben to explain the purpose of the workout, which, like so many of the things I've done here, is unlike anything I've ever done on my own.

"It's just another session that falls under the high-end aerobic category," he said. "When I was running with the Hansons, they had us do a ton of this stuff in marathon training, and I thought I got a lot out of it. I've seen the same results with the runners I coach. There are any number of ways you can slice it—four times two miles, two times four miles, three times three miles—but the general idea is to do a reasonably large volume of work at an effort that's a little harder than marathon effort. I like it because it's fast, but not so fast that you can't keep it up for a while. If you do enough of it, actual marathon pace starts to feel easier. In my opinion, too many runners, even pro runners, train for marathons the same way they train for 10Ks, except with long runs added in. They do mile repeats at 10K pace and say it makes marathon pace seem easier. Well, sure it does—for a few miles! But a marathon is twenty-six point two miles. It's a different animal."

"Guilty as charged," I said.

Marlon Roudette's infectious club banger "Everybody Feeling Something," my chosen theme song for the fantasy I'm currently living, blared through the Fun Mobile's open windows at an inappropriate volume for eight o'clock in the morning as I pulled up next to Faubs's Outback and Veronica's Nissan Versa in the dirt parking area adjoining Lake Mary Start, as it's known. We were soon joined by Matt, Amy, Steph and Ben Bruce, Rochelle, Coach Ben, and my companions from Sunday's long run—Sarah Crouch and Bob Tusso. It has come to my attention in the three days that have passed since Bob's and my first encounter that he is something of a personality in the Flagstaff running scene, a universally liked and ubiquitous man-about-town whose nickname is a play on his surname: Too Slow. Only in Flagstaff is a 2:45 marathoner called Too Slow.

During the warm-up Bob made a seemingly casual inquiry about my workout, which I described with the zealousness of a religious nut seeking converts.

"Mind if I jump in with you?" he asked.

"Not at all," I said. "But don't you have a workout of your own planned?"

"Uh, yes and no."

Back at the parking area, the ritual change of footwear was performed, everyone swapping out trainers for racing flats, and this time I took part as well, having cadged a pair of Hoka Tracers at Run Flagstaff last week.

"I think I shot my wad in the warm-up," I joked, addressing Ben Bruce, who sat on his rear bumper with one ankle crossed over the opposite knee, lacing a shoe à la Mister Rogers. "I don't know how I'm going to get through the actual workout."

"Me, too," Ben said, disregarding my tone. "Seriously. Some days, just getting out of bed is so hard I want to be done with it."

"I know what you mean," Faubs chimed in. He was standing nearby shaking a freshly mixed bottle of Maurten, a high-tech sports drink not yet available to the public that the team is testing. "I have days when I want to go down for a nap and never wake up."

"Jesus Christ!" I said.

Truth be told, I wasn't quite so appalled by my teammates' morbidness as I pretended. Having been with them almost four weeks now, I've gotten used to the gallows humor that is routinely traded among the guys especially. Professional running is a relentless grind, no matter how much you love the sport. Two runs a day, seven days a week, forty-eight weeks a year, plus all the other stuff: strength training, tortuous massages, PT appointments, a burdensome need for sleep. For these folks, voicing the occasional unserious suicidal ideation just might be the only alternative to quitting for real.

As the slowest runner, I again had the honor of starting first. When I was double-knotted and ready, I gave Coach Ben the nod and he and Bob and I moseyed up to the stenciled yellow "S" that marks Lake Mary Start—the first of the sixty-four paint daubs Ben and Jen touch up every spring.

"Do we go when you tell us to or do we just go?" I asked Ben.

"Go!"

We went, Bob keying off me as I keyed off my watch, remembering the promise I'd made to Coach Ben after my last run on Lake Mary Road to not run faster just because I could. And I meant to keep it—I really did. But 6:25 per mile felt so laughably easy that, when Too Slow became restless and began stretching the invisible gangline between us like a sled team's alpha dog, I allowed myself to be pulled along. We hit Mile 1 in 6:14, at which point Bob sped up even more and I reluctantly let him go.

"Too fast, Too Slow!" I called after him, pleased with my cleverness.

I completed the second mile a few paces behind Bob in 6:07, still feeling as relaxed as a tanned man in a hammock sipping from a tall glass of iced tea. Coach Ben was waiting for us at the two-mile mark with my bottle, which I grabbed on the fly.

"What was your time?" he called after me.

"Just a hair fast!" I fudged.

Bob and I jogged side by side for half a mile and then started the second rep. He pulled away from me sooner this time and finished several seconds before I did. Again Ben waited with my bottle, and again he asked for my time.

"Twelve twenty-four," I confessed.

His head dropped. I was supposed to have run 12:50.

About a third of the way into repetition number three, I realized that Bob, although a few strides in front of me, was no longer running faster than I was. I sensed the tables turning, and, sure enough, over the next three-quarters of a mile I slowly eased past him. By the end of the rep, which I completed in 12:12, Too Slow was far enough behind me that I no longer heard his footsteps. Glancing back, I saw him dashing down a grassy embankment toward a stand of trees—the nearest privacy. Poor Bob.

"Time?" Coach Ben asked, again holding out my bottle.

"I feel great and my Achilles is holding up!" I deflected.

Ben laughed despite himself.

When I reached Mile 7.5 and the start of my final repetition, my workout buddy was nowhere in sight, so I took off alone. I was cruising toward a 5:59 mile and really feeling my oats when Matt and Faubs flew past, leaving me behind at about the same rate a scampering child leaves behind a dropped mitten.

"I hate you guys!" I shouted at their backs.

Only in the last half mile of the workout did I begin to feel a touch of heaviness in the legs. But my breathing remained under control, my energy abundant. The phrase *Lake Mary Magic* popped into my head.

When I reached Coach Ben this time I stopped, having completed my morning's work, save for the cooldown, for which I would await a two-pounds-lighter Bob Tusso.

"What was your last mile?" Ben asked.

"Five fifty," I wheezed. Ben's face froze.

"Is that even possible?" he asked.

"Apparently so," I said.

66 Days to Chicago

Another Bagel Run, another chance to talk shop for an hour with Coach Ben as we lagged behind the group. Ben is careful not to be too chummy with his runners, but I've thwarted his efforts to treat me just like any other member of the team by saying things to him that none of the real pros would, and I did so again as we skirted past the looming white bubble that is Walkup Skydome, NAU's big sports arena.

"I have to say, you've assembled a really good group," I confided. "I don't just mean athletically, but character-wise as well. I like every single one of them."

"Thanks," Ben said. "I put a lot of emphasis on that in the recruitment process. There are a lot of talented young runners out there, but I look for guys and girls who will strengthen the team dynamic."

We looked both ways and dashed across Pine Knoll Road toward a trailhead for Sinclair Wash.

"If I could build a team around just one of them, though," I resumed, "it would be Scott Fauble."

"Oh, yeah? Why's that?"

"Because he's a freaking animal!" I said. "That look in his eyes, when he's really grinding? It's like he's about to kill and eat something. Or someone."

Ben laughed noncommittally, neither endorsing nor disputing my judgment. Just then my watched beeped and we turned around. Four miles down, four to go.

"Oh, I talked to Asker Jeukendrup this morning," I said in approximately the same tone one might say, "I tried Nutella for the first time this morning."

Dr. Jeukendrup is arguably the world's foremost authority on endurance sports nutrition, the author of more than 300 scientific papers, and a consultant to the likes of former world-record holder Haile

Gebrselassie. I've picked his brain a few times over the years, and, with Ben's permission, I reached out to him recently to ask if he would be willing to help me dial in my fueling plan for Chicago.

"Oh, good. What did he say?"

"He gave me some homework," I said, choosing my words carefully. "He wants me to send him information about my weight before and after every long run, plus data on temperature, humidity, and elevation; what and how much I drink; and even how much I pee. The part that affects you is that he also wants me to practice drinking on the same schedule I will in Chicago, and obviously I'll need some help with that."

"No problem," Ben said. "Just give me the specifics and I'll pass them along to Ian or Veronica or whoever's handling your bottles that day."

I felt my whole body relax, as though a loud noise I was bracing for never came. A lot of coaches are territorial and take a dim view of what they perceive as outside interference. Ben doesn't seem to be one of them. In a book he wrote for high-school cross country coaches, the revealingly titled *Tradition, Class, Pride*, which I read prior to coming here, he wrote, "It's really healthy for a runner to hear about the sport from new angles not covered by their regular coaches."

"By the way," I said, remembering another question I'd meant to ask, "is my long run on Saturday seventeen miles or nineteen? It says seventeen on Final Surge, but when I add up the parts, it comes to nineteen."

We went over the parts together: two-mile warm-up, four miles at 6:35 per mile, eight miles at 7:20 per mile, four miles cutting down from 6:35 to 6:00, one-mile cooldown.

"Huh," Ben said. "I guess that does add up to nineteen. Well, then: nineteen it is."

"That means I'm going to finish the week with eighty-seven miles!" I said, jubilant. "I haven't logged this kind of mileage in years. How much higher do you think you'll have me go?"

"Not a lot. What *will* change is not so much the number of miles but their consistency. You'll be doing longer, marathon-specific workouts. You can run a great marathon on eighty-five miles a week if they're the right kinds of miles."

"I sure hope I run a great marathon," I said, meaning *a sub-2:40 marathon* but still reticent to speak the number. "Have you considered what might happen if I totally crush Chicago? My blog is getting some traction. Aging dreamers like me will be beating down your door to get you to coach them!"

"Well, there are worse problems, I suppose," Ben laughed. "But that's not why I'm doing this. I'm not looking to be that world-famous genius coach everyone looks at like some kind of oracle. There was a time when I kind of thought I *should* want that, but not anymore. I've come to realize I'm just not that guy. When it comes down to it, I'm not a genius who knows all the science. I'm a culture builder and a motivator. And I'm okay with it."

The other day Matt Llano told me something about Coach Ben that I hadn't known. Five years ago, he took a huge risk, selling his stake in a successful running retail store in St. Louis and moving his family to Flagstaff, where he hoped to make a go of being a full-time elite coach despite having few connections here and no reputation to speak of. Genius or not, he made a good first impression on some of the top local runners, including Matt, whom he started coaching the following year. Around the same time, the one existing professional running team in town, coached by Greg McMillan, lost its sponsor and disbanded. Ben took on some of its former members (among them Ben and Steph Bruce) and before he knew it, he had an elite group of his own, but no funding. Over the course of 2014, he and Jen dumped $40,000 of their savings into the team—pretty much all they had. The couple was a few short steps away from food stamps when Hoka came on board in January 2015.

Not all great coaches have larger-than-life personalities or prodigal IQs, but in my experience, all great coaches give everything they have to their athletes. Ben Rosario just happens to have done this quite literally.

65 Days to Chicago

Shannon Thompson receives her clients in a borrowed meeting room located inside NAU's Lumberjack Stadium. A sports psychologist affiliated with both Hypo2 and the university, she has worked with several members of NAZ Elite, including Matt, whose birthday party she attended the other night. Seated near each other, we had a lively conversation about whether one needs to be slightly crazy to be a successful runner, and though Shannon made no overt effort to press her services on me, I left the restaurant with an appointment. So it was that I found myself seated across from her this afternoon at one end of the giant conference table that dominates her make-do workspace.

"I have three types of clients," she began. "Some athletes come to me because their coach made them. Others have a specific problem they want help with. And the rest aren't really sure what I can do for them, but they're open to various possibilities. Which type are you?"

"Well, as Matt mentioned when he introduced us," I said, "I'm here in Flagstaff to experience the life of a professional runner. Like any real pro, I want to do everything I possibly can to improve, and I believe that working with you is one of those things."

A laptop sat open on the table in front of Shannon. She squinted at the screen briefly before turning her attention back to me.

"Did you get the athlete introduction questionnaire I emailed to you?" she asked.

"Yes. I filled it out and sent it back to you yesterday."

"Really? I don't remember seeing it." Shannon bit her lower lip as she searched her inbox. "Ah! There it is. I'm so sorry. I really need to get more organized."

I took a mental stab at guessing Shannon's age. Thirty-five, maybe? Everyone in this town, it seems, is at least a decade younger than me.

"If you don't mind," she said, shutting the laptop decisively, "I'll look at this later and maybe we can talk about it when we meet again."

I didn't mind. In fact, I felt I'd already gotten something out of answering the form's (literal) twenty questions, each of which invited introspection in one way or another.

3) What about you might cause those who love you to be concerned?

I push myself very hard and I burn the proverbial candle at both ends. I suspect that some of the people I love, my wife and my mom especially, worry that I will push too far in one direction, or that my motives for pushing are not entirely healthy.

Near the end of the form (Question #19), I was invited to name the question I'd most like to be asked when Shannon and I met. She now asked me this very question, her lips cocked in a mischievous smile that let me know she had not read my mind but had simply glimpsed my answer in her brief scan of the form.

"What am I most afraid of?" I repeated. "Failure. No, scratch that. What I'm most afraid of is letting my fear of failure ruin this experience. There's a lot at stake for me here. If I run poorly in Chicago, or if I don't even make it to the start line—which is all too likely given my history—it will be more than just another disappointment for me personally. I'm not doing this for mere ego gratification. I really want to inspire other runners to see how far they can go with whatever amount of talent they have. But nobody will be inspired if I hit the wall in Chicago and finish in three nineteen."

"That's a lot of pressure," Shannon said.

"Which I accept. After all, the real pros are under tremendous pressure, too. Running pays their bills. I want to taste that kind of pressure because I think it has the potential to bring out the best in any athlete. I just don't want to make the mistake of worrying so much about how it all turns out that I miss out on the journey, on simply being here and living this incredible opportunity, because it's the only thing that will matter when I'm ninety years old and all I have is the memories."

"I understand what you're saying," Shannon said, removing her elbows from the vast slab of wood separating us and sitting back. "One thing I would suggest—which may seem counterintuitive—is that you don't even try to suppress these fears you're having. I don't know how familiar you are with eastern philosophy, but from this perspective, perhaps the best thing you can do is accept your fears and observe them without judging. You may find that by doing so consistently whenever they come up, they lose their hold over you. Does that make sense? Or did I just totally weird you out?"

"No, not at all!" I said hastily. "My older brother Josh is Buddhist, so I get the whole mindfulness thing. And it makes sense. I mean, shoot—how can fear *ruin* my experience if I embrace it as an integral *part* of the experience?"

"Exactly!"

After glancing at her phone to check the time, Shannon proposed that we begin to work on a mental performance plan, a tool she uses with all her clients because the one thing every athlete wants, ultimately, is to perform well. Receiving no objection from my side of the eighteen-seat table, she opened her laptop again and fiddled around until she had the right document in front of her.

"First of all, tell me about your best race," Shannon said, facing me again. "The reason I ask is that a good mental performance plan is not one-size-fits-all. In order to help you, it has to be based on *you*—you at your best. So, what does that look like in your case?"

My first thought was that I had never run a "best race," which is half the reason I'm here in Flagstaff. But as I cast my mind back over my twenty-seven-year racing history, I realized something.

"Now that I consider it," I said, "almost all of my best races have been surprises. They were races I went into with modest expectations that I exceeded. But every time I've started a marathon feeling one hundred percent ready to crush it, I've fallen apart."

"That's interesting," Shannon said, glancing again at her phone. "Unfortunately, we're going to have to continue this another time. I've got another client coming in two minutes."

I reviewed the appointment in my mind for the rest of the day. Not until I was winding down for bed with the corrective exercises AJ gave me (which are actually kind of relaxing) did I make the connection between the fear I'd discussed with Shannon and my fear of sharing my Chicago Marathon time goal with anyone. If I'm serious about not letting fear ruin this experience, I realized, I'm going to have to put that number out there. When I do, those three digits will acquire one more layer of meaning and become a symbol of not being afraid to be afraid.

64 Days to Chicago

For a fleeting moment this morning I felt what it's like to be a world-class runner—not a good-for-his-age runner who happens to be training like a world-class runner in the company of world-class runners but a bona fide elite myself, a genetic lottery winner at the height of fitness. It happened on Lake Mary Road, my new favorite place on earth to run, midway through another lunker of a workout: a nineteen-miler with eight easy miles wedged between a four-mile tempo and a four-mile cutdown. I was alone and in the zone, clicking off 96-second quarters with metronomic steadiness, when I began to experience my body in a way I never have before, a hard-to-describe sort of weightless potency that felt almost like flight. My feet did not so much land on the asphalt beneath me as tap it. My lungs seemed suddenly to possess oceanic capacity, as though with one great inhalation I could suck in every last molecule of air from the vast open day around me. I pictured myself striding beautifully down the middle of a broad urban avenue, chasing a crowded press truck flanked by two flashing police motorcycles, the Kenyans trailing far behind me. *This is it!* I thought. *This is what the real pros have—and now I have it!*

Just then I heard footsteps approaching from my rear. Moments later, there they were, the usual culprits, Matt and Faubs, gliding past me, inexorable as aging. Within a few short minutes they were out of sight up the road. I still felt good, but not *as* good.

Mile 8, my finish line, came into view minutes before I reached it, marked by two or three vehicles and a cluster of humans. Faubs and Matt stood sipping from squeeze bottles, done for the day. Sarah Crouch, who'd just wrapped up a solo workout, awaited her husband, Michael, a 2:21 marathoner coached by Ben. The other Sarah, Sarah Cotton, had her ever-present video camera trained on me. And Coach Ben himself counted out loud as I bore down on the cluster, having completed the first three miles of the cutdown in 6:28, 6:13, and 6:01, and now letting it all hang out.

"Five forty-five," Ben droned, "five forty-six, five forty-seven."

I slowed to an unsteady walk and laced my fingers together on top of my head, breathing in huffs. Forgetting about Michael for the moment, Sarah Crouch stalked after me like a zealous Capitol Hill reporter demanding comment from a passing senator.

"Dude, I'm telling you," she said almost angrily, "you're going to run 2:35 in Chicago!"

An hour later, back at Matt's house, Nataki and I had just sat down to plates of baked tilapia with sautéed okra and zucchini when my phone signaled the arrival of a new text message. It came from Sarah, who, evidently, wasn't quite done with me:

Okay, here's the thing, Matt. You've come up to Flagstaff to train like an elite runner, and that's exactly what you're doing physically. But mentally, pro runners set massive goals. Matt Llano said he was fit enough to run 2:08–2:10, and people thought he was crazy. And sure, he ran 2:12, which is kind of a "shoot for the moon and you'll land among the stars" scenario. But landing among the stars is far better than floundering around on planet earth looking up at the sky and just wondering. I honestly believe that if you are hitting your goals more than 10% of the time, your goals aren't ambitious enough. I get that it's scary to put a time goal out there, but you have to have one in front of you to chase. There is a reason that 2:29 is written at the top of every page of my running log. I'm training FOR that.

I'm training TOWARD that. The guy I saw finish that workout today is NOT a 2:40 guy. I couldn't have done the workout that you did today. I just want you to go all in mentally, obsessively, to pick a crazy, unrealistic time goal and just chase it like there is no tomorrow every day for the next 9 weeks, not because you're writing a book, not because I said so, but because this may be the only window in your life where you are able to do that without distraction. Okay, rant over. Recover well, you smashed it today.

I try to avoid texting during meals with Nataki, but in this case I couldn't hold back. Setting down my fork, I let my fish cool as I thumbed out a reply.

I appreciate this, Sarah, not only because it's good advice but also because you care enough to offer it. And I am receptive. My only resistance comes from my sense that there's impossible and then there's IMPOSSIBLE. The idea that I could run 2:35 at age 46 in my 41st marathon after running no better than 2:41 in the previous 40 marathons and no better than 2:49 in nine years is, to me, reality-defying. But my intention is to leave not one scintilla of my potential unrealized on the streets of Chicago on October 8th, whatever that translates to time-wise. Thanks again for the rant.

I know Sarah well enough already that I did not expect her to allow me to have the last word, and I was therefore wholly unsurprised when my phone chimed again barely a minute later. But I, too, like to have the last word. And so . . .

Sarah: Not a big fan of that i-word, ha ha! If someone had told you a month ago that you would run what you ran today, you may have said that was impossible too. I just have that delightful spine-tingling feeling that you are going to surprise yourself in October, whatever that means time-wise. Heck, it may be 85 degrees and neither of us breaks 2:40. Who the hell knows? Anyway, I just like you and want you to succeed, that's what it boils down to.

Me: We will continue this conversation. It would be kind of cool to beat you. . .

Sarah: Bring it, buddy.

Me: That settles it, you're going down!

Sarah: We need to work on our trash talk.

Me: There's time.

Last night I was trying to muster the courage to publicly share my personal goal for the Chicago Marathon, a goal that scares me. Less than twenty-four hours later, a professional runner I met less than two weeks ago is all but forcing me to do precisely this and more. In life there are some people who just have your number. But Sarah Crouch has *my number.*

62 Days to Chicago

I got a second blood draw today—the one that will determine whether training at high altitude is actually working. In truth, I already know it's working because I'm running well and feeling great. Still, I'm curious to find out to what extent the lab results explain my improvement. Have my hemoglobin and hematocrit levels increased a lot or just a little? I'll know in a day or two.

As with the first blood draw, I went straight from the phlebotomist's office to the site of the team run, which was Woody Mountain Road on this occasion. Also like last time, I made a joke about the patch of gauze that was affixed to the crook of my left elbow.

"Just so you know," I said to Faubs and Ben Bruce, "this is from a vitamin B12 infusion. That's my story and I'm sticking to it."

A number of high-profile athletes, among them baseball star Rafael Palmeiro, have at one time or another blamed a failed performance-enhancing drug test on tainted B12 shots. Ben caught the reference.

"It's funny you say that," he said. "I just had an argument about doping with my mom."

The disagreement began, evidently, when Ben expressed skepticism about the validity of Ethiopian runner Almaz Ayana's astonishing forty-six-second victory in the women's 10,000 meters at the World Track and Field Championships two days ago. Assuming the role of devil's advocate, Mrs. Bruce suggested that perhaps it wasn't drugs but a special East African genetic advantage that accounted for Ayana's dominance in London. Her son then countered that there were seven other East African women in the race, all of whom got their asses handed to them by Ayana.

"It's just hard to believe," he grumbled.

Later, during the run, I trotted out the same B12 joke for Steph, Rochelle, Amy, and Kellyn, sparking another exchange on the topic du jour. The object of suspicion this time was Justin Gatlin, a sprinter who recently came off a four-year suspension for performance-enhancing drug use and who, now thirty-five years old—ancient for an elite sprinter—just won the men's 100 meters at the world championships.

"People say, 'Well, he served his time,'" Steph lamented. "What they don't understand is that steroids change an athlete's body forever. Even if Gatlin isn't using drugs now, he's still benefitting from having done them in the past."

I told my companions about an interview I did with Justin back in 2006, in which he told me, "I think that people who feel they have to use drugs and manipulate their fans are criminals." Two months later, he tested positive for testosterone and steroids.

"I was shocked," I said. "He seemed so earnest and conscientious. I learned that you just never know."

Too late, I realized I'd put my foot in my mouth once again, insinuating that my suspicions encompassed *all* elite runners, present company included. But the slip went unnoticed, Steph moving on to share her take on *Icarus*, a newly released documentary film by comedian turned investigative journalist Bryan Fogel, who somehow managed to embed himself with the sketchy (and largely Russian) characters behind international sports doping. No one else having yet seen it, Steph explained in some detail what she had learned from the movie about how cheaters beat doping tests. Kellyn, Rochelle, and Amy were full of questions—the kinds of questions you'd ask only if you'd previously had absolutely no idea how cheaters beat drug tests.

Before I knew it, I was only half listening, distracted by the sudden recollection of a weirdly charged exchange that occurred between Coach Ben and me at the end of our first meeting at Kickstand Kafé four weeks ago. We had just finished discussing the small matter of my goal for Chicago when Ben, the last bite of his chorizo burrito balanced on his fork, asked if I had any more questions, unwittingly handing me an irresistible opportunity to deliver a line I had planned days earlier.

"Just one," I said. "When do I get my EPO?"

Ben dropped the utensil and looked me dead in the eye. *Oops.* I swallowed hard, scrambling for words to undo the words I'd just spoken. Seconds passed like hours as my coach's gaze held mine. I was on the verge of prostrating myself in contrition when, seeing what he needed to see, he let me off the hook, his lips bending into a wry smile.

"Ha ha, very funny," he said.

I had the distinct impression then that if Ben had discerned during those few seconds of unbearable silence that I was not 100 percent kidding around—that if even 1 percent of me genuinely assumed, as many fans of the sport of running do, that all of the top pros are doping, including Ben's athletes, or that I was even 1 percent inclined to accept a few vials of erythropoietin and some syringes from him if he'd had them to give—he would have told me to get the fuck out of his sight and go back to California and never speak to him again.

61 Days to Chicago

Last night several members of NAZ Elite and a handful of their significant others got together at Tourist Home, a popular local hangout, for a patio dinner hosted by Josh Cox, who's in town to present the terms of the team's new contract with Hoka. The atmosphere was somewhat less convivial than it ought to have been, fouled by a vague awkwardness that affected our party of twelve like a bad smell whose source could not be politely acknowledged. On everyone's mind but nobody's lips was the jolt we'd received a few hours earlier, during a two-hour, PowerPoint-illustrated meeting at Flagstaff Aquaplex (a fancy swimming facility with lots of amenities, including meeting rooms), where Josh delivered the news that, for budgetary reasons, the team roster would be pared from thirteen runners to ten under the new deal.

It made me heartsick to know that three of the deserving young athletes seated around me would soon get pink slips. But my heart is only so big, and as the meal wore on, the preoccupied look I shared with the real pros at the table had less and less to do with who would no longer have a job in January and more and more to do with a matter that affected me more personally, and far more imminently, which was the next day's workout: seven times one kilometer at threshold pace on a minute's rest followed by a 1,500-meter time trial.

It wasn't the Ks that scared me but rather the time trial. I hadn't run an all-out 1500 since my junior year of high school, and I'd certainly never run one on tired legs at 7,300 feet. I like to think I can suffer as much as any runner, but that all-out effort promised to hurt in a way I'm not accustomed to. What's more, Faubs and Matt would be doing the very same workout, which meant I would essentially be *racing* them over those closing 1,500 meters. In an effort to take my anxiety down a notch, if only by giving veiled expression to it, I took advantage of Coach Ben's position to my immediate right, probing his expectations.

"So, what's your prediction for my 1,500 tomorrow?" I asked offhandedly, as though this were one of several equally random questions I might have tossed out just for the sake of conversation.

I've been told that Ben is a man who can't resist a wager, and his reaction to my question validated the hearsay. Setting his cheeseburger down, he shut his eyes and massaged his temples, suddenly far more interested in the little parlor game I had proposed than in the next bite.

"I really need to be in front of a computer to do this properly," he hedged. "But for now I'll say five fifteen."

"That seems a bit slow to me," I said, privately elated by Ben's pressure-reducing lowball estimate. My personal goal was to break five minutes.

Later, back at Matt's place, I received a text message from Ben, who evidently had consulted his computer: *Sub 5*.

Just like that, the pressure was on again. But good news awaited me this morning at Mountain Shadows, a development of newer homes situated on Flagstaff's northwest outskirts that happens to contain a flat, horseshoe-shaped street of precisely 1,500 meters' length. The moment I stepped out of Matt's Range Rover (for once we carpooled), Coach Ben informed me he'd successfully recruited Bob Tusso to serve as my workout partner. Happy for the company, I was happier still at the prospect of perhaps not finishing the time trial dead last after all. A few minutes later, Bob showed up wearing the same long-sleeve royal-blue-and-yellow Boston Marathon commemorative shirt that I was wearing.

"I see you got the memo," I said (because one of us had to).

The team warmed up in the forest that surrounds Mountain Shadows on three sides, Ben Bruce entertaining the rest of us—and taking my mind off my nerves—with a lengthy paean to the TV game show *The Price Is Right*.

"Playing miniature golf on television to win a car is my life's dream," he said at one point, his tone so perfectly deadpan that I couldn't rule out the possibility he was completely serious.

The first part of the workout went off without a hitch, Bob and I taking turns setting the pace and averaging 3:35 per kilometer, well below our target. Having started five minutes behind us, Matt and Faubs closed the distance between our pairings with machinelike steadiness, torpedoes hunting tugboats, yet it wasn't until we'd reached the homestretch of the final rep that I heard their footsteps. On a sudden impulse, I launched myself into a full sprint, driving my arms as if a gold medal were on the line, leaving an unconcerned Too Slow to be overtaken by his equally disinterested chasers inches from the finish cone, where I flipped around and backpedaled with my arms raised in mock victory.

Expecting laughter, I got nothing. Not even a smile. Only then did I recognize my mistake: These guys *hate* losing, and while we all knew I hadn't really beaten them, my spontaneous hijinks had touched a sore spot, and they now couldn't fucking *wait* to pulverize me in a true, fair competition.

After three minutes of recovery—time we spent walking in lazy circles, hands on hips, lungs playing catch-up—Coach Ben sent us all off together. Faubs and Matt exacted instant revenge, putting two steps on me with every step, if that's even possible. Tuning them out, I focused instead on executing Ben's instructions, which were to run the first 400 meters in eighty-two seconds and then speed up, a reasonable plan given that the course started with a 600-meter false flat into the wind and then got easier. Bob fell off quickly, but I sensed this only vaguely, my attention rooted on that first cone, which I passed at seventy-nine seconds, already sucking wind. I'd gone a full month in Flagstaff without ever *really* feeling the scarcity of oxygen. Now, all of a sudden, I felt like a lip-hooked trout thrashing on a cement dock, gills fanning desperately, coming up empty.

Midway to the next cone, I saw Ben Bruce loping along on his own up ahead. Still dealing with his abdominal strain, he'd paced Matt and Faubs through their first 400 and then let them go. The closer I got to him, the surer I became that he would jump in with me, a service that a part of me desired, for the motivating effect it would have, and another part feared, for the burden it would put me under not to implode. I caught up to Ben at precisely 800 meters (split time 2:38), and, sure enough, he fell in beside me. "Let's go," he said. "Time to pick it up."

Expertly, Ben settled into a pace that was perfectly modulated to pull me along without quite dragging me over the edge. By this point my brain was so far gone to hypoxia that I had no idea how far I had run, which cone was next, or if I still had a chance of breaking 5:00. But Ben had that covered, too.

"That last four hundred was a seventy-five," he said when we reached the next cone. "Kick it in! Come on! You have less than a minute to go!"

With these well-chosen words Ben peeled away, leaving me to fight my own battle. Ahead I saw the receding forms of Faubs and Matt racing toward a huddle of people (Coach Ben, Jen, Sarah Cotton, one or two others) waiting at the finish. They seemed very far away, like shore to a drowning man. My breathing had become a shrill cry for air, something between a siren and a scream. But I embraced it, all of it, and the nearer I came to that beckoning last cone, the harder I pressed, as if pain itself, not time, were the true measuring stick.

"Four forty . . . *eight*," Coach Ben intoned matter-of-factly when I reached the finish cone, like he'd expected it all along.

Four forty-eight! Four freaking forty-eight! I wanted to pound my chest like a gorilla, cackle madly, quote Muhammad Ali, dance a jig, and pick a fight—all at once. And I just might have, if Faubs hadn't run 4:08, Matt 4:19.

Back at the vehicles, post-cooldown, I slid my Boston Marathon shirt back on and also the raggedy old cargo shorts I wear over my running shorts to virtually every team run (a homely contrast to the stylish team-issue warm-ups the others wear). I was working the zipper on the latter garment when I noticed Craig smirking. I glared at him: *Out with it.*

"Dude, what's up with the cargo shorts?" he asked.

The long answer was that I didn't own any NAZ Elite warm-ups and I didn't want to ask Coach Ben or Josh Cox for another handout and I didn't want to show up to workouts wearing warm-ups with the wrong brand name on them. But I went with the short answer.

"Remember, Craig, I'm a fake pro, not a real pro like you. Gotta look the part."

60 Days to Chicago

This afternoon I sat down at a glass-topped table on the back porch of Matt's house with Andrew Cooper, a student athlete at Washington State University whom I met at last week's Bagel Run. Andrew hosts a podcast aimed at his fellow college runners and is always looking for people to interview. His main interest, naturally, was the real pro in the house, who went first, impressing me (I listened in) with his deft handling of a curveball question about how he keeps his teeth so white. When his promised forty five minutes were up, Matt fled the patio and I took his place before a microphone that looked like it belonged in a recording studio, complete with pop guard.

"What's it like to train for a marathon with a team of professional runners?" Andrew began. "It must be brutal."

"I honestly, not really," I said. "It's hard, but I'm enjoying myself so much that I don't really notice how hard it is, if that makes any sense."

Andrew narrowed his eyes skeptically, but he didn't press, instead moving on to the topic of my background. I told him the same story I told Sarah Cotton about running the last mile of the 1983 Boston Marathon with my dad.

"How about your mother?" Andrew asked cautiously. "Is she still—?"

I cut him off, practically leaping across the table to assure Andrew that my mom is alive and well, saying nothing about the stroke she suffered two years ago. It was a mild one, as strokes go, triggered (according to her neurologist) by a medication she took for chronic migraines. A change in prescription has so far kept a second stroke from occurring, but her short-term memory has deteriorated markedly of late. Any stranger who talked to her at length would think she has moderate dementia, yet the tests say otherwise, and the prevailing theory in our family—what we choose to believe, anyway—is that the symptoms are related to cumulative brain trauma caused by the migraines themselves, nothing too serious.

In the evening, acting on a hunch, I looked up Andrew's website and dug into his own background, learning from a page titled "My Story" that his father had suffered a stroke during Andrew's senior year of high school, two months after Andrew won the state cross country championship, and died weeks later. "My dad loved my running," he wrote. "I'm extremely grateful that I was able to accomplish something great for him while he was alive. Losing my dad made me realize how valuable life was and how important it is to attack every living moment."

I stared at these last words for a long time. *Attack every living moment.* Like a surprise blow to the back of the head, Andrew's account of a parent's premature passing knocked the scales from my eyes, forcing me to see other possibilities. In two days I will fly to Portland, Oregon, to celebrate my parents' fiftieth wedding anniversary with my family. We've gathered there every August for the past three years, a tradition that, for me, always includes participation in the High Street Hustle, a 5K/8K road race held in Salem.

Before today, my thoughts about the trip were selfishly focused on this race, my first chance to really test the fruits of living the life of pro runner. Now I just want to see my mom.

57 Days to Chicago

I felt like an unwilling streaker—naked in every sense of the word—as I performed an improved but still clumsy rendition of B skips in the shadow of the Oregon State Capitol before the start of this morning's High Street Hustle. In fact, I very nearly *was* naked, clad in the skimpy racing kit of Northern Arizona Elite, shorts hemmed a good three inches above my tan line. But it was more than just the paucity of fabric on my body that made me self-conscious. Skimpiness notwithstanding, the uniform I wore was recognizably that of a major professional running team, and as such it drew interested looks from some of the speedier runners drilling and striding around me. Had I been sporting a sumo wrestler's loincloth or Tom Brady's game-day armor, complete with shoulder pads and helmet, I would not have felt any more conspicuous than I did, a feeling exacerbated by internal echoes of a text message Coach Ben sent me last night as I lay on an inflatable mattress in a guest room in my brother Josh's home nearby: *Make that uniform proud tomorrow!*

The blast of the start horn brought a perverse kind of relief, a welcome transition from mental discomfort to physical effort. Tuning out the surrounding stampede, I focused on settling into a pace that I perceived to be just below "the line," as Coach Ben calls it, which is to say a tad slower than the swiftest tempo I believed I could sustain for five kilometers. The temptation to consult my watch was strong, but I resisted for the first 700 meters, a straight shot down Court Street, stealing a glance only when I turned left onto High Street. The number I wanted to see was 5:18, give or take. The number I did see, with a pinch of annoyance, was 5:24.

No sooner had I shaken off this small irritant than I was confronted with a bigger one: The Hill (as Hustle veterans refer to it), a dome-like momentum-crusher rising fifty-four feet over a tenth of a mile that I remembered well from past encounters. Respecting Ben's line, I let gravity have her way with me, albeit grudgingly, ruing the lost seconds. On the far side I was waved through a tree-shaded intersection by a yawning policeman who looked as though he'd rather be just about anywhere else. Hearing my watch chirp, I checked my split for the first mile and cursed out loud, wondering how the hell it was even possible that a 5:31 mile on fresh legs at sea level felt no easier than the 5:47 mile I ran a week ago in

Flagstaff at the end of a huge workout undertaken at the end of a huge week of training.

Scott Fauble's voice now entered my head, speaking the words he spoke to me at Walnut Canyon the other day when I asked him what it's like to race at low elevation after training at altitude, as he himself had done two weeks earlier: *You know, it's funny. You might think it would feel easier, or at least different, but it doesn't. You can just push harder.*

We'd see about that.

The remaining distance to the halfway point consisted of a long false flat, one of those annoying 1 percenters that ramp up just enough to slow you down without seeming like they ought to. The terrain did at least offer the compensating advantage of high visibility, which I exploited to take stock of the competition. Of the five runners strung out ahead of me, three charged right past the traffic cone that marked the 5K turnaround, identifying themselves as participants in the longer 8K event. The next two, both teenagers, circled the cone, identifying themselves as my opponents.

Knowing exactly who stood between me and victory, I shot a mental harpoon at the back of the second-place runner and hauled him in, patiently though, still conscious of the line. I'd just put the kid behind me when my watch beeped again, like a video game marking a kill. I took another quick peek and discovered I had run the second mile in 5:30, one measly second faster than the first, and I said another bad word.

Then I remembered Matt Llano's advice, given to me two nights ago, on the eve of my flight to Portland. I was upstairs with Nataki, trading foot massages, Matt alone downstairs, binge-watching *Parks and Recreation*, when I texted him on a whim to ask how I should approach my upcoming race.

"It's simple," he wrote back. "Just run faster than everyone else!"

At the time I took this response as a glib brush-off. But here in the heat of battle I understood what Matt really meant. For professional runners like him, race strategy truly is as simple as making sure everyone else is behind you when you cross the finish line. Not so for us amateurs, who just try to run as fast as we can, not faster than everyone else—a wholly different mindset. In his own way, Matt was challenging me, asking, *Are you here just to* train *like a pro, or are you willing to* race *like one, too?*

Something inside me snapped. Defying Coach Ben's caution to wait for the top of The Hill to make my move, I punched it on the approach, attacking the sucker like a motocross racer hitting a launch ramp. As I came over the summit, the leader returned to view, closer than before, and a predatory instinct took hold of me, transforming the pain of my burning windpipe into sadistic pleasure, the exquisite agony of the straining cheetah closing in on her fleeing dinner.

Back on Court Street, some 500 meters from a finish line already visible in the far distance, I caught the little bastard. Mindful of our thirty-year age difference, I pressed even harder as I made the pass, hoping to shatter the young man's will and forestall a neck-and-neck sprint to the finish, which I was sure to lose, judging by past experience. Running now with the fear of the hunted rather than the malice of the hunter, I put everything I had into the last tenth of a mile, my head flung back and my mouth gaping, not believing the race announcer when he announced my name to the waiting crowd, declaring me the winner of the 2017 High Street Hustle 5K even as I continued to grope toward the line.

But he was right; I did win. And if I was looking for proof that training with the pros was working, I now had it. My finish time of 16:54, a course record, marked a 44-second improvement on my runner-up performance last year, and I'd covered the last mile of the race in 5:02, the fastest single mile I've run in competition in fifteen years.

Coach Ben phoned me a couple of hours later, by which time I had demolished a Starbucks breakfast sandwich on the way back to Josh's house, taken an extra-long shower, and attired myself for the afternoon's anniversary celebration.

"Take me through it," he said, having learned the outcome already from a tweet I'd posted.

I took Ben through it, harping on the negatives, especially my mistake of running too far under the line in the first two miles and thus missing an opportunity to record a faster finish time.

"But you won!" Ben protested.

"Yeah, I know," I sighed. "I guess I'd still rather lose fast than win slow. You might need more than thirteen weeks to beat the amateur out of me."

53 Days to Chicago

In my twenty-seven years of running I have experienced more than a few runner's highs, but none surpassing the sublime rush that stole upon me this morning on Lake Mary Road, an ecstasy of mind, body, and spirit that combined an intoxicating sense of inexhaustible vigor, the delight of blowing away my most sanguine performance expectations, the joy of running in a postcard-worthy environment, and the pinch-me thrill of experiencing all of this as part of a professional running team. I was on pace to close out what was inarguably the beastliest run I'd ever attempted with a 5:30 mile, having already knocked out a four-mile steady-state effort, a set of four half-mile repeats, a two-mile critical-velocity segment, and a set of four 400-meter sprints. Still visible on the road ahead was Stephanie Bruce, who had started the same workout two minutes behind me and who—surprised perhaps by how long it had taken her and pacer Nick Arciniaga to hunt me down—had chided me for running too fast when she finally slid past me ("Sorry, Steph," I replied, not sorry). Gratitude swelled my heart to the brink of bursting as I entered the last quarter mile, a rapturous rush of thankfulness for the gift of being here, now, doing this.

ZAP!

A white-hot bolt of pain ripped through my groin, on the left side, at the crease between leg and crotch. Time slowed, as it does in the moments before an automobile collision. I knew something terrible had happened, but a stubborn instinct goaded me to keep running, to finish what I was so tantalizingly close to finishing. In any case, I was running too fast to have stopped instantaneously even if I'd wanted to, and when my left foot touched down again a second white-hot blast of pain triggered the same sequence of mental events: raw animal recognition of grievous bodily damage followed by a mulish insistence on continuing despite it.

A third shot to the groin brought me to my senses. Picturing soft tissue separating from bone, I staggered to a hitching walk, my mind weirdly empty, numbed by the dawning realization that it was all over. My fake pro runner fantasy was gone, just like that. There would be no sub-2:40 marathon. Not in Chicago, not ever. My last best chance to achieve a goal I'd hungered after for more than a third of my life had vanished in a flash, and at the precise moment it seemed most within reach.

Like a dazed soldier seeking the source of his bleeding, I probed the fingertip-size epicenter of pain radiating from my loins with a pair of fingers as I limped toward the spot where Jen Rosario (standing in for her husband, who was on a plane to Kuala Lumpur to support Rui Yung Soh, a Singaporean elite, in the Southeast Asian Games Marathon) waited with my drink bottle and a timer. I'd covered about a third of the remaining distance when Ben Bruce and Craig Lutz came jogging my way from Jen's direction, having completed their workout.

"What's the matter," Ben joked, eyeing the hand on my crotch, "did you break your penis?"

Something in my face caused his smile to drop.

"Are you okay? Do you want us to have Jen bring the truck?"

I waved away the offer.

"I can walk," I said lifelessly. "Go ahead and finish your cooldown."

By the time I came within speaking distance of Jen, my 5:30 mile had turned into a 7:30 and-counting mile.

"What happened?" she asked.

"Hurt my groin," I said. "It's bad. I think I tore something."

Jen handed me my bottle, as she would have done anyway, the mute gesture somehow communicating a sympathy she lacked words for. I received the Maurten-filled plastic cylinder mechanically, contemplated it for a second or two, then raised my arm overhead and slammed it against the pavement, punctuating its impact with a primal curse.

"Stay calm!" Jen pleaded. "I'll text Ben."

While Jen thumbed away at her phone, I paced back and forth, my thoughts racing. What the hell was I supposed to do now? Hang around Flagstaff for another seven and a half weeks, unable to run, pitied by everyone around me until their pity ran out? Unthinkable. Go home to California, to the prison of old routines, marking time until some new adventure came along? Whoopee.

"Ben wants you to see AJ or Wes as soon as possible," Jen broke in, "and let him know what they tell you."

"I have an appointment with AJ this afternoon," I said, my voice once again drained of emotion. "It was supposed to be for my Achilles, but—well, whatever."

I climbed into the front passenger seat of Jen's truck for the ride back to Lake Mary Start. Faubs, Nick, and Futsum—whom Jen had quietly made aware of my misfortune when they returned from their cooldowns—squeezed into the back.

"Don't jump to any conclusions," Faubs said from behind me. "These things sometimes seem a lot worse at first than they turn out to be."

I knew better than to reach out for the lifeline of hope Faubs was tossing me. Nothing in my vast catalog of experience with injury encouraged it, and I understood all too well what hoping in hopeless situations gets you. But I grabbed hold anyway, powerless to resist the feeble succor of magical thinking.

We arrived at the dirt lot where everyone had parked, and the truck emptied out. I opened my door only to discover that Jen had edged too close to a ditch to allow egress on the right side of the vehicle. The obvious solution was to slide over to the driver seat and exit from the left, but this required that I raise my injured leg, which I couldn't do. Too prideful to ask for help, I extricated myself by using my hands to lift my leg like a construction crane hoisting a beam, then slunk to the Fun Mobile unnoticed as my teammates traded stories about their workouts.

ABOVE LEFT: I captured this selfie with my Flagstaff host, Matt Llano, to memorialize Day One of my fake pro runner adventure. *Courtesy of the author.* ABOVE RIGHT: Brothers AJ (blue shirt) and Wes Gregg (red shirt) needed to give me a lot of direction in my first strength workout with NAZ Elite. Olympic miler David Torrence, who died tragically a few weeks after this photo was taken, is in the background. *Courtesy of Sarah Cotton.* BELOW (Left to right): Scott Smith, Aaron Braun, Scott Fauble, Ben Bruce, me, Matt Llano, Stephanie Bruce, Futsum Zeinaselassie, Kellyn Taylor, Craig Lutz, Rochelle Kanuho. *Courtesy of Jen Rosario.*

ABOVE LEFT: If memory serves, I was in the middle of saying "How ya like me now?" when this photo was taken one mile into a long workout on Lake Mary Road. I had nailed my first split (for once) and was feeling pretty good about myself. *Courtesy of Sarah Cotton.* ABOVE RIGHT: The Arizona Trail at Snowbowl, elevation 9,000 feet, is just one of many impossibly beautiful places to run in and around Flagstaff. *Courtesy of Sarah Cotton.* BELOW LEFT: A few days after I suffered my groin injury, I huddled with Coach Ben (center) and AJ Gregg (right) to map out my path back to full training. *Courtesy of Sarah Cotton.* BELOW RIGHT: I took this shot of Futsum and Craig, running way faster than I ever could, after warming up with them at Buffalo Park. *Courtesy of the author.*

ABOVE LEFT: Bob "Too Slow" Tusso and I shared many miles together during my time in Flagstaff, including this one at Mountain Shadows. *Courtesy of Sarah Cotton.* ABOVE RIGHT: Before my very first run with the team, I learned this strap assisted hip flexor stretch from Matt Llano, and I continued to do it for the next thirteen weeks. My dog, Queenie, sometimes supervised. *Courtesy of Sarah Cotton.* BELOW LEFT: Queenie became fast friends with Matt Llano's dog, Harlow, during the three months Nataki and I spent in Matt's home. *Courtesy of the author.* BELOW RIGHT: Eric "Big Dog" Fernandez was pulled out of his retirement from professional running to serve as my occasional workout pacer. *Courtesy of Sarah Cotton.*

ABOVE LEFT: More than once, Ben Bruce (right) turned a negative for him into a positive for me by running with me on days when his injury kept him from running at his normal speed. *Courtesy of Sarah Cotton.* ABOVE RIGHT: I caught Aaron Braun demolishing a Krispy Kreme donut minutes after he completed a 22-mile depletion run. (I myself ran 22 miles and skipped the donuts.) *Courtesy of the author.* BELOW: A little less than halfway through my stint as a fake pro runner, I made a trip to Salem, Oregon, to celebrate my parents' golden wedding anniversary and to run the High Street Hustle 5K, which I completed 44 seconds faster than I had the year before, gaining important proof that my fake pro runner experiment was working. *Courtesy of GCC Photography.*

ABOVE: Although their personalities are very different, Stephanie Bruce (left) and Kellyn Taylor were equally fun and inspiring for me to be around for 13 weeks. *Courtesy of Ben Rosario.* BELOW: In the waning weeks of my time with NAZ Elite I made a few trips with them to Camp Verde to train at lower elevation. *Courtesy of Ben Rosario.*

ABOVE: While in Flagstaff I made a friend for life in James McKirdy, seen here pacing me through a workout on Lake Mary Road. *Courtesy of Sarah Cotton.* BELOW: Taking part in an annual adult running camp hosted by Steph and Ben Bruce (right) helped me take my mind off my groin injury. Scott Fauble (seated) served as a counselor. *Courtesy of Sarah Cotton.*

ABOVE LEFT: Although she wasn't a member of NAZ Elite, elite runner Sarah Crouch did more than anyone I met to get me thinking (and dreaming) like a pro. *Courtesy of Sarah Cotton.* ABOVE RIGHT: Two weeks before the Chicago Marathon, I enjoyed my last sip of alcohol with James McKirdy at Majerle's Sports Grill. *Courtesy of Heather Szuba.* BELOW: Racing the Chicago Marathon in the elite division gave me the privilege of putting whatever I liked into eight self-selected drink bottles that I would (barring mishaps) find waiting for me at 5-kilometer intervals along the course. *Courtesy of the author.*

TOP LEFT: On the first leg of the trip from Flagstaff to Chicago I found myself seated next to 2016 Olympic Marathon winner Feyisa Lilesa of Ethiopia. *Courtesy of the author.* ABOVE RIGHT: I dropped nine pounds during my time as a fake pro runner. Here I am on race day, weighing 141 pounds, the lightest I'd been since high school. *Courtesy of the author.* CENTER LEFT: When I called my parents after completing the Chicago Marathon, my dad told me, "I saw you on TV!" Here's proof. *Courtesy of Anthony Molinaro.* BOTTOM LEFT: Midway through the Chicago Marathon, I was on pace to achieve my goal but worried about an untimely recurrence of pain in my recently recovered groin. *Courtesy of Cindy Kuzma.*

Two hours later I was in AJ's office, lying faceup on the treatment table with my legs in a figure four, right leg straight, left leg bent and hinged outward. Having heard my account of the incident, AJ now sought a diagnosis, pressing down gently on the inside of my knee to assess the ability of the hip abductor tendons (AJ's more exact term for *groin*) to stretch. He might as well have jabbed me with a letter opener. The muscles along the inner thigh clenched in automatic resistance and AJ yanked away his hand as though scalded.

"Okay, now try pushing against my hand," he said. "As hard as you can."

I pressed my knee into his palm, AJ adjusting his counter-pressure to match my force and keep my leg from actually moving.

"Does that hurt?" he asked.

"Not much," I said.

"Okay, go ahead and sit up."

I sat up, AJ straightening my leg for me with the gentleness of a hospice nurse assisting a goner.

"So, what's the verdict?"

"I think it's highly unlikely you tore something," AJ said in his usual tone of monkish serenity. "We'd need an MRI to be certain, but I'm pretty confident it's just a severe case of acute tendonitis. That's a two-week injury. It will heal, I promise. But you may need to adjust your expectations for Chicago."

Another lifeline. I clutched this one, too, almost hating myself for my inability to do otherwise.

AJ described my treatment plan: high-dose ibuprofen, alternating applications of heat and ice, a half dozen new rehab exercises, and daily lasering. After demonstrating the exercises, AJ ushered me over to a seat nearer the cold laser machine, which he switched on with a practiced no-look finger flick.

"Due to the location of the injury, I'm going to have you run the laser on yourself," he said primly, handing me the wand.

"Any danger of singed pubic hairs?"

"Actually, yes," AJ smiled. "You wouldn't be the first."

Coach Ben's promised call came at midafternoon, catching me lounging in boxer briefs at Matt's house with a newly bought heating pad wrapped around my upper leg.

"Bring me up to speed," he said sleepily. It was 6 A.M. tomorrow in Malaysia.

Conscious of how quickly the thing that had happened on Lake Mary Road was becoming *the story of* the thing, I repeated to Ben everything I had already told AJ, but with more polish, concluding with AJ's diagnosis and treatment plan.

"Let's take three days off," Ben said with characteristic decisiveness. "And I mean *off*. No running, no cross-training, nothing but rehab. And don't do that runner thing where you test it five times a day."

I laughed guiltily, having done this once or twice already.

"I know it sucks," Ben said, "but I've seen the three-days-off trick do miracles. When Eric Fernandez was training for CIM last year, he hurt himself doing the same workout you just did. He was convinced it was another stress fracture. I had him take three days off, and guess what? The next time he ran, the pain was gone. When it's all said and done, you might look back at this as nothing more than a speed bump, and I'm not just saying that. I believe it."

A third lifeline of hope offered, a third taken.

I spent the balance of the afternoon updating my blog. No sooner was the news of my "broken penis" posted than I began to hear from my new friends in Flagstaff. Big Dog sent me a direct message on Twitter, inviting me out for a consolatory beer. Too Slow emailed me to extend his sympathies. Sarah Crouch texted me with orders to get my ass down to Flagstaff and see John Ball. Steph went so far as to call me up and invite me to participate in any and all non-running activities on the itinerary of her annual adult running camp, which begins tomorrow, as a way to distract myself from my situation.

"Stay positive," she exhorted. "You can't control everything, but you can control that much."

After the call, I went back online and scanned the comments being left on my social media feeds by runners who, though strangers to me, had become personally invested in my journey as a fake pro runner, folks who wanted me to succeed not just for my sake but for the sake of what my success might mean for them, and who were now gutted by my failure.

I just wanted to reach out and say I'm sorry this happened. You were living the dream and you help so many of us live ours.

Oh, man. So sorry to hear this. As a 45-year-old, living vicariously through your experience was hugely inspirational. Get well soon.

Clearly well intended, these commiserative expressions only widened the circle of my disappointment. In the past, I failed only myself in failing. But this time I've also failed everyone who had a stake in my success. Or have I? My brain says *yes*, my heart says *maybe not*.

Don't jump to any conclusions. These things sometimes seem a lot worse at first than they turn out to be.

It will heal, I promise.

When it's all said and done, you might look back at this as nothing more than a speed bump.

Stay positive.

There's no going back now. Hope will either see me through this thing or betray me once again.

51 Days to Chicago

Shannon could tell something was wrong the moment I sat down across from her at the same humongous conference table we'd communicated across in our first appointment. Perhaps it was my slouched posture, or maybe my subdued tone. I suppose I might as well have been wearing a sign.

"What is it?" she asked.

"I'm injured," I said. "Shredded my groin in a workout on Wednesday. Coach Ben's not letting me run for three days, and as you can imagine, I'm losing my fucking mind."

"Oh, no!" Shannon said, smiling incongruously. "That sucks. I'm so sorry."

"It sucks on many levels," I sighed. "Obviously, my goal is in jeopardy, and that sucks. But I've been in this position before, more times than I care to remember. What's different this time is that I'm *here*. I've never enjoyed running more than I am enjoying it now and not only because I'm running well. *Was* running well. I just love being with the team, and I miss it already. Regardless of what happens with this injury, I go home in seven weeks, and it's killing me that I'm missing out on an experience that's going to end so soon."

"That's understandable," Shannon said, no longer smiling. "One thing I always encourage my clients to do is turn obstacles into opportunities. That can be difficult if you're *just* an athlete and you get injured and you can't achieve a goal because of it. But you're *not* just an athlete—you're also a writer. Who knows? If you're open to it, maybe you'll end up with a story that's even more inspiring than the one you would have told if you hadn't gotten hurt."

This was perfectly sensible advice, but it was predicated on the assumption that the death of my dream was a fait accompli, and I'd snatched up too many lifelines of hope to accept this just yet.

"Yes, I am a writer," I said evenly, "but I'm still an athlete. And, as an athlete, I don't want to let go of my goal. If I can't bounce back from this thing and run well in Chicago, then, sure, I'll need to find a way to write about my experience that somehow makes lemonade from lemons. But I'm not ready to give up. I want to fight!"

"I love it!" Shannon laughed. "Even as an athlete, though, you can turn this into an opportunity. I'll give you an example. My brother Tyler is a rock climber and also a drummer. Last year he broke his right foot during a climb—the foot he uses to play the kick drum. While he was recovering, instead of not playing at all, he used his left foot instead. And guess what? When he was able to use his right foot again, he played better than ever!"

I got the gist of the story, but I didn't quite get the take-home lesson, so I asked Shannon to name the running equivalent of drumming left-footed. She suggested visualization: doing exactly the same workouts I would be doing with the team if I were healthy but in my head instead of with my body.

"I know it sounds crazy," she said, "but there's actually some science to suggest it might be beneficial."

"I guess I could try that," I said.

"You don't sound too enthusiastic."

I closed my eyes briefly, searching for the right words.

"I just can't believe it's come to this," I said. "Running in bed wasn't exactly what I had in mind I when I came here."

50 Days to Chicago

I was back in AJ's office, lasering my loins for the fourth consecutive day, when the question I knew was coming and didn't want to answer came.

"What's your report?"

"Oh, it was fabulous!" I said with an overbright smile. "Nataki ordered the venison and I had the flank steak. We shared a salad of baby artisan greens with beets and fennel root and a cold smoked salmon tartine. Everything was divine. I would put The Cottage right on par with Coppa Café. You're two for two!"

AJ has been my go-to source for restaurant recommendations since he helped me break my streak of bad choices for Friday date night by steering me to Coppa and a couple of other places.

"That's great," AJ laughed. "But I meant the report on your groin."

"Ah, yes, of course," I said, giving up the act. "Well, it hurt a little when I walked with Nataki this morning."

"Then you're not running tomorrow," AJ said flatly.

The question of what happens after today—my third and last day of enforced rest—has been on my mind almost constantly since Coach Ben imposed the hiatus. Ben himself has said little on the topic, in part because he's still in Kuala Lumpur but also because, in situations like this, it's the doctor or physical therapist (or chiropractor, in AJ's case) who assumes the role of coach, guiding the athlete through rehabilitation toward "return to play," as it's called. What's certain is that I will take up some form of cross-training tomorrow to preserve my fitness while I ease back into running. It's the running piece that is unresolved. During yesterday's appointment, AJ and I discussed the possibility of my testing the groin with a short walk/run session tomorrow, contingent on the report I delivered today, which, as I had feared, AJ had given a failing grade.

When the lasering was done, AJ put me back on the treatment table and repeated the same tests he'd used to diagnose the injury. I bent my left leg sharply and swung it out to the side like a dog watering a fire hydrant. AJ then applied gentle hand pressure to the knee, his eyebrows raised inquisitively. I shook my head, so he applied a little more pressure. I shook my head again and AJ pressed down even harder.

"Huh," he said. "Your range of motion is back to 100 percent."

I pounced.

"What harm can it do me to run for a few minutes tomorrow, really slow, just to see how it feels?" I asked.

"None, as long as you stop right away if there's pain above a three out of ten. You might even find that running loosens it up a bit. But to be straight with you, I'll be happy if you're running again in eight days."

In the afternoon, I returned to Hypo2 with Nataki for a classroom session with attendees of Steph's running camp. The subject of her talk was mental toughness.

"What I love about running is that it's the only part of life where you get to choose how much you suffer," Steph told the gathering. "And the more you are willing to suffer, the greater the reward."

Ben Bruce chimed in from the wings: "It's kind of a messed-up sport."

"It *is* messed up," Steph agreed soberly.

A camper named Amanda raised her hand and asked Steph what she tells herself during difficult moments in a race.

"Well, I'm a huge Rocky fan," Steph confessed, lightly blushing. "I think maybe it's because Sylvester Stallone reminds me of my father. Anyway, I usually think of lines from Rocky movies. For example, in *Rocky IV* there's the part where Rocky draws blood from Ivan Drago and his trainer tells him, 'See? He's a man just like you!'"

At yesterday's talk, held at Moses Cone Park, Steph shared her story, somewhat unnecessarily, as most of the campers are huge fans of hers and likely knew it already. Raised in Phoenix, she started running early—we're talking preschool-early—and displayed an immediate and obvious talent for it. Yet something in her, perhaps a lack of self belief, kept her from fully committing to the sport. In high school, Steph mixed running with a fast food–heavy diet and a fair amount of weekend partying, much to the chagrin of her father, James, who told her time and again that she could be truly great if she would only honor her gift.

Adding urgency to these paternal appeals was the fact that James was slowly dying of prostate cancer, a disease that landed him eventually in hospice care in New York City, where, on February 15, 2002, an eighteen-year-old Steph traveled to say goodbye. Before visiting the hospital, she squeezed in a run on Long Island, during which she experienced what she could only describe to us as "a weird feeling." Upon returning to the home where she was staying, Steph learned that James had died at the precise moment of this weird feeling.

The loss affected her deeply, but not entirely negatively, especially where her running was concerned. As if James's belief in his daughter had somehow transferred itself to her upon his passing, Steph began to aim higher and dig deeper. Come spring, she lowered her mile time from 5:27

to 4:58 and finished second in the state championship—and the rest is history, as they say.

To close out her talk, Steph picked up her phone and played a snatch of audio from her favorite scene in *Rocky Balboa*, where Rocky delivers some tough love to his son, Robert, after Robert tries to talk his father out of stepping back into the ring at age sixty.

"Let me tell you something you already know," Rocky says in that marble-mouth baritone. "The world ain't all sunshine and rainbows. It's a very mean and nasty place, and I don't care how tough you are—it will beat you to your knees and keep you there permanently if you let it. You, me, or nobody is gonna hit as hard as life. But it ain't about how hard you hit; it's about how hard you can *get* hit and keep moving forward. How much can you take and keep moving forward. That's how winning is done! Now, if you know what you're worth, then go out and get what you're worth. But you gotta be willing to take the hits, and not pointing fingers, saying you ain't where you want to be because of him, or her, or anybody. Cowards do that and that ain't you! *You're better than that!*"

Unexpectedly, and almost to my embarrassment, a righteous anger began to bubble up inside me as I listened, Rocky's words enflaming the smoldering frustration I've carried the past few days. My mind began to cast about for enemies, targets of my sudden lust for vengeance. It didn't take long. Yesterday I received an email message from a self-described fan of my writing who wanted me to know that he and some of his training buddies had placed bets on how long I would survive with Northern Arizona Elite before I got injured, and that he had won the wager, having chosen the exact date of my groin injury. His delight in my downfall was obvious, despite cursory efforts to sandwich his gloating between trite expressions of sympathy.

It's a mean and nasty place . . .

When the meeting broke up, I burst from the room as though I were stepping outside a bar for a fistfight, my entire body buzzing with adrenaline, or testosterone, or some other ass-kicking hormone, my inner Rocky delivering some tough love to my inner crybaby as I limped along, my groin pinching warningly.

Are you just gonna lie down and allow this asshole and everyone else who expects or wants you to fail to laugh in your face? Or are you gonna find a way to make it to Chicago despite what happened, and despite whatever else might happen, and run the time you want to run, and RUB THEIR GODDAMN FACES IN IT?

They call it bulletin-board material—you know, "Tell me I can't and I'll prove that I can." The real pros use it routinely as fuel for great performances. Why can't I?

49 Days to Chicago

Nataki and I were enjoying an al fresco brunch at Josephine's, an upscale bistro that sits on tier two of AJ Gregg's local restaurant rankings, when my phone buzzed, the screen lighting up with Coach Ben's name and number. After a slight hesitation, I went ahead and picked up, a breach of etiquette I privately justified by the fact that the call was coming from Malaysia, not to mention that it concerned a matter of far greater importance than my fellow diners' desire for freedom from telephonic intrusions: my groin.

"Still remember how to run?" Ben asked.

"It's like riding a bike," I said.

Today was the day. I woke up early, tingling with the same nervous anticipation I feel on race days, though the test in front of me was about as unrace-like as a run could possibly be. One part of me wanted to march straight down to Matt's garage and learn my fate (AJ had insisted the session be done on a treadmill), while another part wanted to put off the moment of truth as long as possible. So I compromised and stuck to my normal schedule, consuming my usual granola-and-coffee breakfast and then returning to the bedroom to ice and heat my groin and bang out my daily rehab exercises.

At quarter to eight, while Brauny, my fellow Chicago Marathon entrant, was getting ready for a long run on A1 Mountain Road that would have been on my schedule as well if I hadn't gotten hurt, I changed into running gear and made my way toward the garage, still inwardly divided, half of me approaching the Precor C964i like a five-year-old scampering toward a merry-go-round, the other half dragging his feet like a condemned man being led to the electric chair.

AJ and I had agreed on a protocol at his office yesterday: twelve minutes of slow jogging broken into two-minute segments separated by walking bouts of equal duration. If at any point my pain level exceeded a rating of three out of ten, I was to stop immediately.

My right index finger tremored visibly in its wavering search for the machine's START button. I set the speed to 3.0 miles per hour, or about dog-walking pace, and eased into motion, my eyes glued to the time readout as though it were the countdown clock on an explosive device. After two minutes I stabbed the SPEED ↑ button eighteen times in quick succession, gently transitioning from walking to jogging as the treadmill belt accelerated beneath my feet, my attention concentrated marksman-like on the afferent feedback signals emanating from the bull's-eye of my injury.

Immediate discomfort triggered a moment's alarm, but my fright soon passed as I realized what I was feeling wasn't pain so much as the threat of pain—perhaps a two on AJ's ten-point scale—and it held steady at this level until it came time to walk again. My relief was great but incomplete, like that of a Russian roulette player who hears the click of an empty bullet chamber knowing he has another turn coming.

The pain climbed another notch—nosing right up to AJ's limit—during the next jogging bout, and before I knew it I was praying, not to a higher power but to the injured tendon itself, pleading with it to spare me a second show-stopping nail-gun shot like the one I experienced out on Lake Mary Road. It worked. Or maybe it didn't work, and the credit belongs elsewhere. Whatever the case, I was able to complete the session without any further escalation of symptoms.

Feeling more hopeful, perhaps, than circumstances warranted (the Chicago Marathon is forty-nine days away, I've run a grand total of

1.2 miles in the past four days, and I'm currently unable to run faster than ten minutes per mile), I pressed the STOP button, pulled the power cord from a waist-high wall socket to my right (Matt insists on this after every session), snatched my phone from its perch on the console, and was just about to hop down from the machine when I froze suddenly, contemplating the device in my right hand.

Should I or shouldn't I?

Before I could change my mind, I typed a quick text message to Coach Ben:

I want to run 2:39 in Chicago.

Ben made no mention of this communication during today's intercontinental discussion of my successful test run, nor did I bring it up again. No need. It's out there now.

47 Days to Chicago

So soundlessly did Coach Ben creep up on me that I nearly leapt out of my skin when he addressed me through the Pilot's open passenger window.

"How's it going?"

AJ had cleared me to run outside today: thirty minutes total in five-minute chunks. It was hardly worth driving somewhere for, but Ben (who's finally home from Southeast Asia) wanted to see me run, so he asked me to show myself at Kiltie Loop, where Faubs was doing a short fartlek before flying out to Flint, Michigan, to race the Crim 10-Mile.

"It's going okay," I said after recovering from my initial startle. "Still hurts, but not as much."

Ben made no immediate comment, seeming at a loss for words.

"Yeah, but you're running *really* slow," he said eventually.

"Ten-minute pace, to be exact," I said. "My new normal. If I tried to run any faster, it would be a problem."

"Well, I call it a win," Ben said, regaining his customary positivity. "Let me go check on Faubs and I'll get back to you later."

True to his word, Ben ran the last five-minute segment at my side, laying out his plan for me.

"So, here's the deal," he said. "The way I look at it, we've got a couple of extra weeks to play with. Normally, you'd start tapering two weeks out from Chicago, but when you're coming off an injury and trying to regain fitness, that goes out the window. Once you're healthy enough to do real workouts, we'll have you run hard every three days right up until the marathon, and you'll be fine. How does that sound?"

"I like it," I said.

"What's critical is that you get in one solid month where you're able to train full-on. I'm sure people have been telling you that you've got plenty of time, and you do—until you don't. That's just reality."

"Okay," I said, consulting a mental calendar. "Four Sundays out from Chicago is September tenth. That gives me a little less than three weeks to get healthy."

"Chin up," Ben said. "We've seen how quickly you can get fit here."

We had stopped moving by this point and were conversing face-to-face near our parked vehicles. Glancing down at my watch, I realized the timer was still running.

"Crap—I forgot to stop my watch!" I said, jabbing the red button. Only then did I realize how absurd my concern for exactitude was in my present situation. "Ha! Who cares?" I laughed mirthlessly.

"I know, it sucks," Ben said.

45 Days to Chicago

Hearing a vehicle pull in behind me, I paused my stroll across the parking lot at Hypo2 and turned to see Brauny's Subaru slide into the last empty spot. An almost queasy expression came over his face when he got out and noticed me waiting for him, as though I were some wayward second cousin of his who hit him up for money whenever our paths crossed. I took no offense, knowing how awkward it is sometimes to be around an injured teammate. You feel both grateful for and guilty about your own good health, and your instinct is to hide both emotions, an effort that inevitably results in stilted communication. Taking mercy on him, I spoke first as we entered the building together.

"Good workout for you yesterday, eh?"

Aaron posted a mildly self-deprecating tweet after yesterday's 20 x 1K session at Mountain Shadows (another workout I would have done "with" him if not for my injury), evidence to anyone who knows his modest nature that he was well pleased with it.

"It was," he said, trying not to sound too happy. "I felt pretty good aerobically the whole way. My legs just got tired toward the end—kind of like in a marathon, come to think of it, which I guess was the point."

It's a long walk from the front entrance of Hypo2 to the weight room, and there came a point in our journey down the main hallway where Brauny had no choice but to ask about my groin despite my obvious determination to steer the conversation in a different direction.

"I think I'm entering the anger stage of my recovery," I told him glibly, "which is probably a good sign. It means I'm impatient to start running hard again, and I'm impatient because I'm feeling better."

"Been there," Aaron said. "You'll feel a *lot* better once you get to do that first real workout and you see you haven't lost as much fitness as you thought. And then you'll start to see the bright side of taking time off: 'Hey, at least my other aches and pains got a chance to quiet down. And I'm not worried anymore about overcooking myself before the race.'"

Aaron knows whereof he speaks. Imagine being twenty-nine years old, the main breadwinner for a family of four, and realizing your career—the only occupation you've ever known or loved—is probably over. That's where Brauny found himself last year, a mysterious hip injury that defied every treatment known to man, including prolonged rest, having wiped out his

2015 season and threatening to do the same to 2016, an all-important
Olympic year. His Adidas contract was set to expire in a few months.
Aaron wasn't naive. He knew that if he didn't produce some results
before then, he'd be out of a job. Desperate, he went to plan B, applying
for thirty college coaching positions all over the map. Thirty rejections
later, he went to plan C, relocating the family from their longtime home
in southern Colorado to Flagstaff, scoring a last-chance contract with
NAZ Elite, and consulting the oracle of John Ball, with whose help he
has been able to slowly bootstrap his way back to 120-mile weeks. Brauny
and I both have something riding on the Chicago Marathon, but for him
the stakes couldn't be higher.

"Hey, Fitz!" Coach Ben called out as we entered the gym. "We were just
talking about you. What's the good word?"

By "we" he meant himself and AJ, who stood at his side, and the "good
word" he sought was a report on the five-mile run I'd done earlier in the
morning at Fort Tuthill County Park.

"Pain level one!" I said.

AJ promptly handed me a workout sheet that, to my great satisfaction,
included a couple of exercises (kettlebell swings, goblet squats) I'd been
forbidden to do last week—another step forward.

It was a full house. Brauny was already down on all fours in the warm-
up area, doing bird dogs. Next to him, Kellyn cranked out pistol squats
like they were nothing. In the center of the room, Futsum modeled perfect
front-squat technique. Above him, Craig was making hanging leg raises
look easy. Over by the mirrors, Ben Bruce watched his reflection perform
a set of reverse lunges. To his left, engaged in forward lunges, was Maria
Elena Calle, an Ecuadorian native coached by Ben, who qualified for last
year's Olympic Marathon at age forty-one and is visiting from her current home in Virginia for a stint of altitude training. At the very back was
Rochelle, doing goblet squats. And in the far corner, close to the dumbbell
rack, Steph counted off weighted calf raises. But as I scanned the room in
search of a place do my single-leg reverse deadlifts, I became aware of one
notable absence: Amy Van Alstine.

It's not unusual for a team member to miss the occasional strength workout—indeed, both Matt and Faubs were absent as well, but in their cases I knew why (Matt is recovering from the half marathon he did last weekend, Faubs is in Flint for the Crim 10-Mile)—whereas Amy's non-appearance was unexplained. What's more, I realized, I hadn't seen her in some time. I could only hope the reason was something other than a worsening of her own injury.

Three hours later, Coach Ben sent an email message to the whole team under the ominous subject line "Roster Update," and I had my answer. It read, in part, "Amy and I had a meeting earlier this week and we've decided it's in her best interest and the best interest of the team to grant her a release effective immediately . . . The release is completely amicable and there was no incident. After nearly four years with the group she's looking for other options moving forward and having the fall to explore those options is an opportunity we wanted for her."

My mind leapt back to a moment from the team meeting we had two weeks ago, when we learned that three roster spots would be eliminated at year's end. In sharing these grim tidings, Coach Ben had emphasized that no decisions had yet been made concerning who would be let go, but when the meeting broke up and everyone rose to leave the room, I noticed that Amy remained seated, looking as if she'd just seen a puppy get run over by a car. Reading the tea leaves, she must have decided to jump before she was pushed.

This is the other reason it's sometimes awkward to be around an injured teammate.

44 Days to Chicago

Midway through a morning ride on Matt's ElliptiGO (a seatless bicycle I've been using for cross-training), I stopped to pee in one of a pair of portable toilets generously positioned outside Lake Mary Country Store. As I stood over the hole, breath held and phone in hand, I opened an email message that had just come in from Josh Cox, then opened an attached PDF and found myself staring at an elite athlete contract for the Chicago Marathon with my name on it. My stomach did a backflip.

I should mention here that when I arrived in Flagstaff seven weeks ago, I was not registered to participate in the 2017 Chicago Marathon in *any* division, let alone the pro division, having missed the deadline to sign up. On learning of my predicament from Coach Ben, Josh told me not to worry, citing his "great relationship" with race director Carey Pinkowski. True to his word, he got me a bib.

But he didn't stop there. I've known Josh since the early days of his own professional running career, when, acting as his own agent, he landed a role on Season 3 of *The Bachelorette* and scored a number of other lucrative opportunities that are beyond the reach of most 2:13 marathoners. After hanging up his racing flats in 2012, Josh put his persuasive powers to work for other professional runners, negotiating the most generous team contract in the entire sport on behalf of NAZ Elite. Hardwired to get as much as he possibly can for whomever he's representing (even fake pro runners, evidently), Josh went back to Carey Pinkowski and asked him on my behalf to make a one-time exception to the normal qualifying standard for elite males (a recent sub-2:14 marathon time or the equivalent at another distance), arguing that it would be "good for the sport," and good for the Chicago Marathon in particular, if he were to allow an Average Joe (who happens to be a writer) to experience what it's like to compete in a World Marathon Major as an elite.

Back at the house I sat down to study the document, which appeared to be identical in every way to the one Brauny and other real pros had already signed except that it contained no appearance fee and no travel support. Most of its ten pages were made up of mind-numbing legalese, but I found a few interesting nuggets, including a clause requiring, in essence, that I not show up for the race weighing 300 pounds ("Athlete agrees to train, prepare for, start and use best efforts to complete the October 8, 2017, Chicago Marathon").

I couldn't wait to tell people about it, and in the evening I got my chance in the form of an invitation from Maria Elena to join an undefined "us" for dinner at Diablo Burger. At the restaurant, our hostess greeted us with her usual equatorial ebullience, crushing Nataki and me with ferocious embraces that belied her waifish proportions. Rochelle showed up a minute or two later and then Kellyn, trailed by an entourage comprising her husband, Kyle, their daughter, Kylyn, and three of Kyle's relatives. Last to join the party were a couple of strangers (to me): Katja Goldring, a former NAZ Elite member, and her husband, Travis. After placing our orders up front, we migrated outside to a sun-bathed patio seating area and squeezed ourselves into a picnic table whose maximum seating capacity was definitely less than eleven.

All at once everyone seemed conscious of the fact that no single person among us knew every other person, and the conversation got off to a slow start. Seeing an opening, I took full advantage.

"So, I signed an elite athlete contract with the Chicago Marathon today," I announced.

"That's so cool!" Maria Elena gushed. "Congratulations!"

"It's a very interesting agreement," I said professorially. "It made me promise not to use performance enhancing drugs, and I'm now officially eligible to claim prize money. I get $100,000 if I win and another $75,000 if I break the course record of 2:03:45."

"Oh, wow!" Nataki said. "Do you think you can do it?"

Everyone laughed, assuming Nataki was joking, but I knew she wasn't. After twenty years with me, my soul mate knows no more about the sport of running than I do about hairdressing (one of her great passions).

"I think you should at least *try* to win," Nataki said to me later, privately, as we walked to the car. "I mean, why not?"

41 Days to Chicago

When Coach Ben sends out a team email on any day other than Sunday, I've learned, it's more likely to contain bad news than good news. So I was expecting bad news when, as I made my slow way up the switchback staircase at Matt's house on this Monday, ice pack in one hand, phone in the other, I received a team email from Ben, and all the more so because it bore the subject line "Bad News." Heart clenched, I tapped it open immediately, braced for the cold touch of death, praying for something less, *anything* less—bankruptcy, divorce, whatever. But no.

> Team,
> I have some gut-wrenching news. You may already know but our friend David Torrence has passed away. I don't know what else to say. I'm shocked. It's the worst possible news.

Below this brutally economical bit of prose was a link to a report on a *USA Today*–affiliated website that I read on my computer in the bedroom while icing my groin. Thin on details, the brief article raised more questions than it answered, stating only that David was found early this morning at the bottom of a swimming pool at the condo complex where he resided in Scottsdale and that the local police saw no evidence of foul play. The presumed cause of death was drowning.

"*Drowning?*" Nataki repeated when I shared the report. "A thirty-one-year-old Olympic athlete? It just doesn't make any sense."

Hungry for more information, I went to Twitter, where already the running community was beginning to react. Those who knew David shared photos of him and stories about him that, in every case, captured the Category 5 joie de vivre that made me a fan of his long before I met him at Hypo2, where he pronounced himself a fan of mine in a gracious effort to soothe my battered ego after I'd made a fool of myself in my first strength session with the team. Then I thought of Matt.

Knowing just where to find him, I found him there, pacing dazedly between stove and refrigerator, oven and pantry, opening and closing cabinets and drawers randomly with an unfocused look in his eyes.

"Terrible news about David," I said.

Matt continued to pull cooking implements from their storage places and put them back unused.

"I'm in shock," he said eventually.

"How well did you know him?"

"We were supposed to have lunch together in Phoenix on Wednesday."

"Oh, dear. Matt, I'm so sorry."

He said nothing more, so I went back upstairs, but I continued thinking about David for the rest of the day and well into the night, taking a small measure of comfort in the belief that, if he had known even for one second that he was going to die before he did, he would have left this world with few regrets.

What about me? If I died tomorrow, would I go without regrets? I mulled this question over as I lay in bed at Nataki's side, awaiting sleep. A few likely regrets came to mind. Not having been a better husband, for starters. Not having been a better son. A better brother, brother-in-law, uncle, nephew, coworker, friend. Focusing too much on running and writing and not enough on other people.

And, God help me, not having run a faster marathon.

39 Days to Chicago

Nataki and I were munching on turkey burgers at Matt's kitchen table when my phone issued the four-tone jingle that heralds an incoming email message. Still chewing, I peeped at the screen just to make sure it wasn't yet another bombshell from Coach Ben and saw that the sender was my dad, the subject "Your Mom," the recipients all three sons. My stomach dropped through the floor.

I stole a glance at Nataki's face, as though seeking confirmation that the seismic tremor I'd just felt wasn't all in my head. Finding her contemplating her next bite, I opened the message, the mere length of which confirmed my worst fears before I'd read a single word. I must have forgotten to breathe as I sped through my father's carefully chosen phrases, for by the time I'd absorbed the last of them ("We need you to be a key part of this whole deal") I was woozy, gasping. Dropping the phone to the table, I blinked several times to clear my vision and resumed eating, trying my best to maintain a poker face, but without success.

"What's wrong?" Nataki asked. "Did something happen?"

Saying nothing, I flicked my eyes in the direction of the TV seating area, where the newest occupants of the downstairs guest bedroom, Canadian runners Josh and Tanis Bolton, were lounging on Matt's massive sectional, watching one of those critically acclaimed Netflix or HBO or Amazon series that I can't keep straight because I haven't seen any of them. Understanding, Nataki proposed—more loudly than necessary—that we take Queenie for a walk.

"My mom has Alzheimer's disease," I said outside, whispering needlessly. "I just found out from my dad."

Nataki has an admirable yet also heartbreaking way of receiving bad news as though she were expecting it, and this instance was no exception.

"Okay," she said simply. "Let's pray on it."

Nodding assent, I stopped walking, secured the handle of Queenie's leash in my armpit, and offered Nataki my hands. As usual, she led the divine petition, asking God to heal my mother and to give our family peace and strength in the meantime. I mumbled "amen" and thanked my wife for the heartfelt words, but I felt no peace just yet. I wanted to *do* something, not just sit around waiting for a miracle. But what? Nothing came to me.

Then I thought of Steph, who had not only lost her father to prostate cancer as a teenager but whose mother, Joan, was now battling breast cancer. Resuming the walk, I texted her, requesting an immediate audience. Steph's reply—an invitation to swing by her place in the evening, after the boys had been put to bed—came quicker than expected, interrupting my efforts to scoop up a steaming pile of fresh dog doo-doo.

Later, on our way over, Steph texted again, asking us to please *not* ring the doorbell and instead let ourselves in through the unlocked front door.

We did as instructed, tiptoeing like a pair of cat burglars up a darkened stairwell to the main living space on the second floor, the home's quirky layout familiar to me from my one prior visit, which, by sheer coincidence, occurred only this morning, when a small group of NAZ Elite runners met there for an easy run. The home remained in the same state of colorful disarray, the paraphernalia of two preschool children strewn everywhere. Steph greeted us with a token apology for the mess and offered us seats on a sectional that was relatively free of clutter, Nataki and I claiming one side of the L, our hostess the other. In the brief silence that followed these maneuverings, we overheard Ben's efforts to tuck in his sleep-resistant young sons at the far end of the hallway that led to the bedrooms, his words indecipherable but his tone, playfully admonitory, pretty much telling the story. A smiling eye roll from Steph indicated it was more or less the same story every night.

"So, I just found out my mother has Alzheimer's," I blurted.

Steph stiffened as though stunned by a surprise slap to the cheek. Recovering, she began to say the sort of thing you're supposed to say at such moments, but I interrupted.

"I know, it's terrible," I said. "I'm feeling completely gutted, as you would expect. But I'm also feeling a lot of guilt. I mean, here I am wrapped up in this fantasy life as a fake pro runner while the woman who gave me life is facing a death sentence. As a real pro runner, you have no choice but to make running a top priority. But you have a family, too, and your mom is also sick, and it seems to me you do a pretty good job of balancing your priorities. So, what I want to ask you, I guess, is how do I put running first without putting my mom second?"

"I don't think it's a matter of putting one thing first and another second," Steph said. "I try to be the best runner I can be, the best mom I can be, the best daughter I can be, and the best wife I can be at all times. Sometimes it's very challenging, but I'd rather fall short than lower my standards. When my mom was diagnosed with cancer last year, I was training for CIM, logging my biggest weeks. I took an active role in supporting her, but not at the expense of my running. I did workouts right from the hospital in Phoenix where she was being treated if I had to. When it's important enough to you, you find a way."

"That's helpful," I said. Thank you."

"Let me just say one other thing," Steph said. "Don't allow anyone, including yourself, to trivialize what running means to you. It *is* very selfish, but if everyone pursued a passion they loved the way you and I love running, the world would be a better place. Your parents *want* you to be here, doing what you're doing. Make the choices you need to make. If and when it's the right thing to go see your mom or help your dad care for her, you'll know."

While Steph spoke, Ben entered the room quietly and took a seat beside her. By the time she'd finished, he was fully up to speed and ready to offer his two cents.

"Did you ever see the movie *50 First Dates*?" he asked. Nataki and I both shook our heads. "It's just a silly comedy, but it's kind of deep in a weird way. Adam Sandler plays this guy who's in love with a woman who lost her memory, so he has to start over with her every day. What he ends up learning is that all the nice, romantic things he does for her aren't wasted just because she doesn't remember them. I see the same thing with Riley and Hudson. They can have the funnest day ever one day and the next day it's gone, like it never happened—but they're still happy. That's maybe something to keep in mind with your mom."

We talked a while longer, drifting inexorably from the subjects of disease and love and family toward the magnetic north of running. When Steph failed to stifle a yawn, I thanked her and Ben again for their advice and stood, offering my hands to Nataki for the second time today, a day I wish I *could* forget but surely never will.

SEPTEMBER

37 Days to Chicago

I came downstairs somewhat later than usual, whereas Matt rose early, a coincidence that resulted in my finding him already well along in the process of preparing two slices of toasted Dave's Killer Organic White Bread Done Right with organic berry harvest spread when I entered the kitchen. Never one to invite conversation before sunrise, my host pretended not to notice me, but two can play at that game, and I pretended not to notice his desire to be left alone.

"Was it awful?" I asked.

"Huh? Was *what* awful?"

"David's viewing."

Yesterday Matt drove to Phoenix for the second time in two days. The first trip was planned well in advance, a quick sortie down the mountain for an appointment with John Ball that was supposed to have been followed by lunch with David Torrence. But David is no longer taking nourishment, so instead Matt came straight home to sleep and bang out a couple of runs and a strength workout before returning to the valley to say a final goodbye to his friend last night.

"It wasn't easy," he said. "It was different from every other viewing I've been to. Usually people just file through and don't interact much. But this time everyone kind of gathered at the front and people took turns telling stories about David, which was nice. It gave us a chance to laugh and cry and it made the whole thing more cathartic than I expected. But, well, how do I say this? My understanding is that the whole thing came together quickly, and David's going to be cremated, so they didn't, um . . ."

"Prep him?"

"Yeah. He wasn't, you know, wearing a suit or anything like that. It's not the way I wanted to see him for the last time."

I shuddered at the image—David's warm, handsome, olive-tinted, animated face now bloated, waxy, cold, and still.

"So, what have you got this morning?" Matt asked, pointedly changing the subject.

"Fartlek," I said. "My first real workout in sixteen days."

"But who's counting?" Matt laughed.

Life goes on. Three hours later I was warming up with Steph (the only other team member who had the same workout as me: ten times one minute fast, one minute slow) on the wooded trails that branch off Kiltie Loop. Two summers ago, David stayed briefly in Ben and Steph's home, during which time he volunteered as a counselor at their first adult running camp, his playful, people-loving personality making him a hit not only with the campers but also with baby Riley (whose brother, Hudson, was baking in Steph's womb at the time), and he'd remained an honorary uncle to the boys ever since. Aware that Steph, too, had attended the viewing, I waited for her to bring it up, but she didn't, so I asked for her take on the experience.

"It was brutal," was all I got out of her.

Back on pavement, we started the fartlek together, but within ten strides Steph was two strides ahead of me. I couldn't have cared less, so grateful was I to be healthy again (touch wood) and running relatively fast. Coach Ben leapfrogged between us in the Pilot, doing his coaching thing. I was jogging along between my third and fourth reps when he rolled up next to me to check in.

"How's it going?" he asked, his grin revealing that he already sort of knew the answer.

"Remember how a couple of weeks ago you assured me I wouldn't lose much fitness in a couple of weeks? Well, you were right!"

On the drive back to Matt's house, the new Sir Sly song "&Run" came on the radio. Always a sucker for a juicy bass line, I turned up the volume and drummed out the beat on the steering wheel.

"Well, *somebody's* in a good mood," Nataki said.

She spoke teasingly, in allusion to the acknowledged fact that, as my running goes, so goes my temper. But her playful calling out of my unconscious behavior had the opposite of its intended effect. My smile dropped, a wave of guilt dousing the bliss Nataki had caught me expressing. *What kind of monster am I?* I thought. *David Torrence is dead, and I'm happy because my running is improving?* Burning with shame, I sent a psychic note of apology to David's memory—or started to, but then I stopped, realizing that if anyone would understand my joy, it was the man who, while in college, bet his teammates that he would run a sub-four-minute mile before the year was out (his best time to date was 4:07), then measured out a *downhill* mile on Bancroft Way in Berkeley and ran it in 3:46 at two o'clock in the morning.

Life goes on.

35 Days to Chicago

If I hadn't gotten injured, I would have done a sixteen-mile depletion run two weeks ago, consuming no carbohydrates either before or during the session. Widely practiced by elite runners, depletion runs are believed to teach the muscles to metabolize fat more effectively, thereby boosting endurance. I've done depletion runs on my own for a few years, but after Friday's fartlek run at Kiltie Loop I made the unhappy discovery that I've been doing them wrong—or at least not the NAZ Elite way—and I'd have to switch protocols for today's workout, which Coach Ben scheduled as a makeup for the depletion run I missed.

Steph and I had completed the fartlek and were chatting with Coach Ben as we changed shoes for the cooldown when I happened to mention that I was looking forward to eating eggs and sausage today, a breakfast I rarely indulge in except before depletion runs because eggs and sausage contain no carbs. I'm not sure what sort of response I was expecting, but it wasn't the narrowed eyes and cocked heads I got.

"Why are you looking at me like that?" I said.

"You do realize you're not allowed to eat *anything* before a depletion run?" Ben asked. "Black coffee. That's it."

"Really? I've always eaten a zero-carb breakfast."

"That's cheating!" Steph said. "It's way easier!"

"I don't think so," I countered. "Your way might be harder psychologically, but the muscles don't know the difference; they're equally carb-deprived in both scenarios."

"I'm not so sure about that," Steph said.

"Well, if the rule is no food whatsoever, then I won't eat anything—if only to prove you guys wrong!"

When Matt came into the kitchen this morning he found me sipping my coffee glumly. Food is always my very first thought when I wake up.

"I'm so hungry," I moaned, eliciting a knowing laugh from Matt.

"It'll go away as soon as you start running," he assured me. "Then it will come back in the last few miles."

By eight o'clock a large group that included the Flagstaff Long Runs crew was assembled at the base of Road 222, site of my worst run in Flagstaff so far, a not-so-easy easy run I did back on July 21. Within half a mile of setting out, I remembered why I'd struggled that day, the road's relentlessly upward slant and traction-thwarting loose-gravel surface making eight minutes per mile as challenging as six. Seemingly unaffected by these hindrances, the other fall marathoners—Brauny, the two Scotts, Matt, Kellyn, and Steph—who'd been given slightly longer depletion runs, drifted ahead steadily, leaving me behind with Rochelle, Alex Harrison (the young guy who's chasing 2:35 at Chicago), and a stranger who ran with his arms hanging at his sides as though carrying invisible water buckets.

"How far are you going?" I asked Rochelle.

"Six," she said. "I tweaked my back last week doing leg speed."

"I'm sorry to hear that," I said, having in fact already heard about the injury from Maria Elena. "You're far too young for back problems."

"It's my own fault," Rochelle said. "John Ball says it happened because I have weak abs."

"I don't see how that's your fault."

"It is, though. I used to do a ton of core work. I wanted to have a six-pack like Kellyn. But no matter how many crunches I did, my stomach looked the same. So I got frustrated and quit."

"Dang," I laughed, "I thought only us amateurs cared about that stuff!"

At three miles, Rochelle turned around, the road leveled off, and Alex and the guy carrying invisible water buckets sped up, and suddenly I was alone. I soon came to a table Coach Ben had set up for the team. Exactly one bottle remained on it: mine. I snatched it up and took a few swigs of water, Ben shouting out something I didn't quite catch from behind me as I ran on. After two or three sips, I tossed the bottle to the ground, close to where Addison was playing in a ditch. Only then did I notice the plastic milk crate on the road ahead of me, filled with my teammates' water bottles, and I realized what Ben had said that I hadn't quite caught initially.

Drop your bottle in the crate!

A few minutes later, Ben rolled up next to me in the Pilot.

"Sorry about that," I said.

"You're such a diva," he laughed. "'Fetch, boy!'"

No sooner had Ben sped ahead to set up the next drink station than my groin, which had been quiet until then, began to hurt. Having experienced a number of small flare-ups since my initial return to running fifteen days ago, I wasn't worried—at first. But as I ran on, the pain intensified, and my confidence gave way to chagrin, chagrin to dismay, dismay to alarm, and alarm, eventually, to panic. Like a man trapped in a high-rise inferno trying to choose between leaping and burning, I debated whether to stop running or press ahead, certain I was fucked either way. If I pressed ahead, I risked fully reinjuring myself. But if I stopped, I was faced with the reality that just five weeks before I hoped to race 26.2 miles, I couldn't even jog sixteen miles.

In the end, I didn't so much decide to keep going as just kept going. At 7.3 miles I saw Ben again. Handing me my bottle, he broke the news that I would have to carry it the rest of the way, the real pros having gotten too far ahead of me for him to continue leapfrogging. I waved off his apology and assured him I'd be fine on my own, saying nothing about my groin.

At eight miles I reversed direction. Halfway. One more hour of pain to endure. And for what? I was clearly on a degenerative course. I'd seen this movie before and I knew what came next. Even if I survived today, the next workout would hurt more and the next one even more, and so on, until I couldn't run at all. I'd sensed in my gut that my quick recovery from the catastrophe on Lake Mary Road was too good to be true, and sure enough, it was.

Then suddenly I remembered words Ben Bruce spoke to me last Saturday when we bumped into each other at Fort Tuthill and ran together for a spell, discussing our respective injuries. "I still feel it," Ben said in reference to his nagging abdominal strain, "but at the moment it's not stopping me from running, and as far as I'm concerned, that's all that matters." It struck me then how unfailingly the real pros manage to put a constructive spin on the challenges they experience, and I realized now how woefully short of their example I was falling with my present pity party.

What would Ben Bruce—or Kellyn, or Craig, or any of my elite teammates, for that matter—do in my situation? I knew the answer: They would maintain perspective and take stock of the positive. So that's what I tried to do as I winced my solitary way through the inbound portion of the run. I reminded myself that if a magic genie had prophesied immediately after my injury that, just eighteen days later, I would run sixteen miles, albeit in some discomfort, I would have been delighted. And although my pain level was unacceptably high, it was no longer increasing. And, come to think of it, I felt pretty good fitness-wise. Despite skipping breakfast, I was at no risk of hitting the wall.

Aiding these efforts to reframe my situation was gravity, whose helping hand made the last three miles as cheatingly easy as the first three had been annoyingly difficult. When I got back to the Fun Mobile, I quickly demolished the Clif Bar, banana, and Starbucks Frappuccino I'd stashed in back and then waited with Nataki, Rochelle, Sarah Cotton, and Veronica to cheer the return of the professionals. Coach Ben parked the Pilot, hopped out, and came straight over to me to check in.

"Well, how was it?" he asked.

"Easiest thing I've ever done," I said.

33 Days to Chicago

The door to Shannon Thompson's meeting room-cum-office was open, so in lieu of knocking I paused at the threshold and waited for her to notice me, which took a few seconds because she had her nose buried in a book, the old kind made out of paper. Taking my usual seat, I flicked my chin inquiringly in the direction of the slim volume now resting before her on the giant conference table.

"Do you read poetry?" Shannon asked.

"I do," I said. "I also write poetry, if you can believe that."

"I can, actually. Do you happen to know David Whyte? I've been on a big David Whyte kick lately. He's philosophical, but in a down-to-earth way."

I told Shannon that I haven't had as much time to read here as I do at home and that poetry might be just the thing to squeeze into the small gaps between my runs and physical therapy appointments and rehab exercises and whatnot.

"So, what was it you wanted to see me about?" she asked.

I had reached out to Shannon to request an "urgent" appointment after learning of my mother's diagnosis but gave no reason other than to say it wasn't about running. I now gave her the reason, using the same blunt wording I had with Steph, and I got much the same reaction. Shannon's face drained of blood and her jaw went slack, as though I'd just confessed to a murder and asked for her help in disposing the body. For the first time in my three meetings with her, she seemed stumped, and when at last she found her tongue, she admitted as much.

"I don't know much about Alzheimer's," she said. "It's never come up with any other athlete I've worked with or affected anyone I'm close to personally. Honestly, I have no idea how to help you."

"That's okay," I said. "I have people I can talk to about the personal side of the situation. I'm coming to you as an athlete. I mean, the world hasn't stopped. There's only so much I can do to help my mom at this stage, and although I'm determined to do what I can, in the meantime, here I am, still chasing a goal that means a lot to me, still having a once-in-a-lifetime experience. I feel I need to compartmentalize—to focus on running when it's time to run and to focus on my mom when that's appropriate—but I'm not sure if it's even possible."

Shannon stood abruptly, removed a single sheet of paper from a bulletin board hanging on the near wall, and handed it to me before sitting down again.

"I don't really believe in accidents," she said. "I was just telling you that I'm on this David Whyte kick, right? Well, here's a poem of his called 'Start Close In.' I put it up not five minutes before you walked in, and it is exactly the advice I would give anyone in your place but said much more beautifully than I ever could. Go ahead and read it."

The type font was small, and I'm on the verge of needing reading glasses, but by holding the page at arm's length I was able to fulfill Shannon's request.

Start Close In

Start close in,
don't take the second step
or the third,
start with the first

thing
close in,
the step
you don't
want to take.

Start with
the ground
you know,
the pale ground
beneath your feet,
your own
way to begin
the conversation.

Start with your own
question,
give up on other
people's questions,
don't let them
smother something
simple.

To hear
another's voice
follow
your own voice,
wait until
that voice
becomes an
intimate
private ear
that can

really listen
to another.

Start right now
take a small step
you can call your own
don't follow
someone else's
heroics,
be humble
and focused,
start close in,
don't mistake
that other
for your own.

Start close in,
don't take
the second step
or the third,
start with the first
thing
close in,
the step
you don't want to take.

"Wow," I said, laying aside the poem. "I see what you mean. When
I think about it this way, it's obvious what my first step should be, and
that's simply to be there for my mom—to make time for her. It sounds
so easy, but in a sense it really is a step I don't want to take because I've
always been so focused on myself. When I talked to Stephanie Bruce
about this the other day, she suggested I write a letter to my mom every
week. I thought it was a great idea. That was exactly a week ago, and I

haven't even started the first letter. By the way," I added, lifting the paper again, "can I keep this?"

"Yes, of course."

"What advice would you give me right now," I asked, "if there were some rule that forbade you from offering any counsel that did not directly bear on my running performance?"

"Okay," Shannon said, laughing, "I'll play along. Except I'm not going to give you advice. I'm going to tell you a story."

Last spring, she told me, three elite runners came to her individually for advice about personal matters that, like my present worry, had nothing to do with running but impacted their running in one way or another. In the course of working with them, Shannon asked each of these men to tell her about his best race, and she noticed a striking pattern in their answers.

The first client said that his best race was a half marathon he ran two years earlier, in which he achieved a huge PR that astonished everyone, including himself. It was also the first race he'd ever run while involved in a happy and fulfilling romantic relationship. I knew who this runner was, having heard the same story directly from Matt Llano's mouth, but I held my tongue.

The second client's best race was a half marathon also, a race he'd run under immense pressure in a last chance bid to qualify for the 2016 Olympic Trials Marathon. His most vivid memory of the day was from the start line, where he caught sight of his parents in the crowd of specta tors and burst into tears, overcome by gratitude for the support they'd given him and the sacrifices they'd made for him over the years. The other thing he remembered was that the race itself felt utterly effortless, and he achieved his goal.

The third client's best race was a 10,000-meter track race that he contested in a last-chance bid to meet the Olympic qualifying standard for that distance, having never run the required pace for even 5000 meters. Unlike the second client in Shannon's story, this athlete came from a fractured family that had shown little support for his running. But on this occasion his father, who had seldom seen him compete, and his brother, with whom he did not get along, rallied behind him, joining him on a road trip from the town he'd grown up in to the site of the event, a healing experience that made the outcome of the competition seem less important. He ran the time he needed and went to the Olympics.

"There are only two things that are proven to have the power to counteract the kind of pain and fear that athletes experience in competition," Shannon summarized. "One is the flow state, where you are completely absorbed in what you're doing and self-consciousness disappears. The other is love."

32 Days to Chicago

There are sheep in the woods around Kiltie Loop. I wouldn't have guessed it, but there they were, a massive flock of fluffy white merinos swarming the trail from our right flank as we attempted to pass through this morning—Aaron, Craig, Michael Crouch, and I, warming up for a set of mile repeats—blocking our passage with seeming deliberateness. As primates and ruminants converged, my companions slowed, leaving me to cut a path through the creepily silent floe of fleece.

"They're closing in on me!" Brauny called out in mock terror.

"They can smell weakness!" Michael warned.

"In that case," I said, "*I'm* the one who should be worried."

Truth be told, I did not feel weak. In fact, I felt like a god, my freshly shaved legs (about half of the guys on the team manscape) communicating the same youthful snap as before the injury, a frog-like springiness that distracted me from my assorted aches and pains in much the same way a three-beer buzz takes one's mind off a toothache. Having survived the sheep attack, I completed the first of my assigned half dozen repeats—a full circuit of the Kiltie Loop, starting and ending at its southwest corner—in

6:01, five seconds below the target pace Coach Ben had given me, barely breathing. Whatever humility I had gained during my recent injury setback went up in smoke as I clicked off the next two miles, not merely enjoying how good I felt but privately congratulating myself on being a terrific runner.

"You're recovering quickly," Ben observed as I sipped from a bottle of Maurten during a short break between reps three and four.

"I don't even need the recoveries," I boasted. "I could do these straight."

"Listen to this guy!" Ben said, turning away to address an imaginary audience.

Midway through the next rep I met Rochelle, who is easing back toward full training and had already finished her workout—a light fartlek—and begun to cool down.

"Can I join you?" she asked, beginning to turn around.

In hindsight, I recognize that it was not Rochelle's intention to stick a pin in the overinflated balloon of my ego. Nor do I blame her for assuming I was done with my mile repeats and was cooling down also. After all, not a minute earlier, Aaron and Craig had ripped past her with the swiftness of greyhounds, and now here I was plodding along 20 percent slower, heel striking, arms flailing. But in the moment, my pride was wounded.

"I'm still working out!" I yelled.

Recoiling like a startled cat, Rochelle aborted her U-turn and scrambled off in her original direction while I thundered on, my mortification slowly giving way to a grudging appreciation of the humor of my comeuppance.

"You should have heard what Rochelle said to me out there," I said to Coach Ben after completing a pride-fueled 5:53 mile.

"She told me," Ben said, grinning merrily. "She's embarrassed."

"Good," I said. "May she never live it down."

A few minutes later, I returned to the woods to cool down with the real pros. The sheep had vanished.

30 Days to Chicago

I know perfectly well now where NAU Fields are, yet I somehow got turned around on the way there this morning and showed up late—not as late as the first time, when I missed an entire session of drills, strides, and plyos, but late enough to trigger my weird thing about time waste and a tingle of déjà vu as I reprised that day's hair-on-fire sprint across the grass. Only this time it was not Coach Ben waiting for me at midfield but a loose circle of NAZ members arranged in attitudes spanning from diligent stretching (Brauny) to leonine repose (Futsum).

"Who else is coming?" Futsum asked as I joined the circle.

"It was in the email," Craig said, the exasperation in his voice hinting at a long history between them. "But, of course, you don't read the emails."

"Hey, why do I need to worry about what everyone else is doing?" Futsum rejoined. "As long as I know where I'm supposed to be and when, I'm good."

At Walnut Canyon the other day I asked Futsum if his next race was next weekend or the weekend after.

"I'm not sure," he answered.

Accepting defeat, Craig informed Futsum that Kellyn and Michael Crouch were also coming.

"Who's Michael?" Futsum asked.

"He's been here for weeks!" Craig said, incredulous. "You did a whole long run with him!"

Futsum shrugged.

It was déjà vu all over again three hours later, in AJ's office, cold laser blasting my groin for the umpteenth time, AJ and Nataki and I discussing food.

"Are you going to Elote tonight?" AJ asked.

Elote Cafe is a restaurant in Sedona that AJ recommended to us as the best place to eat within seventy-five miles of Flagstaff that we had not already experienced.

"Tomorrow," I said. "Matt told us to get there at four thirty, which is half an hour before it opens, because they don't take reservations and there's always a wait. Nataki and I normally eat dinner at five anyway, so that's not a problem as far as we're concerned."

"You guys are so old," AJ laughed. "What time do you go to bed?"

"Eight o'clock," Nataki said. "But we get up at five. What time do you go to bed?"

"I go to bed at ten."

"And what time do you get up?" Nataki asked.

"Nine."

"That's eleven hours of sleep!" I said.

"I need an abnormal amount of sleep," AJ said glumly. "It's a major inconvenience. But my life goes completely sideways if I don't get it."

"You'll probably outlive Methuselah," I said.

"God, I hope not."

We spent the remainder of the session discussing age, aging, and factors that affect longevity. AJ brought up the much-studied but controversial connection between caloric restriction and increased lifespan. I mentioned the less well-known fact that certain personality traits are associated with healthy aging and longevity.

"Worriers tend to die young," I said, "which bodes well for Futsum, but not so much for me. On the other hand, I've also read that people with strong passions tend to age well. I'm pinning my hopes on that."

"You mean running?" AJ said. "I hate to say it, but at the rate you're going, you might not be running a lot in your retirement."

"That's okay with me as long as I'm still writing," I said. "My father is seventy-four and writing better than ever."

I thought back to my interview with Sarah Cotton, how it brought back the pain I went through when I realized—prematurely, perhaps—that my athletic decline had begun. For as long as I can remember my happiness has been dependent on the feeling that I am ascending—rising higher, getting better, not just as an athlete but in every important dimension of my life. So salient is this feature in my personal makeup that it inspired my brother Josh to dub me Project Matt when I was still in high school. Was it true, then, what I said to AJ? I want to think so. After all, it's not aging per se that I fear but decline. It is almost certain that my running will begin to decline again soon after I leave Flagstaff, but I'd like to believe I'll be okay with this, regardless of what happens in Chicago, as long as I'm still able to ascend in other ways.

"Doctors tend to get worse with age," AJ volunteered.

"That makes sense," I said. "At some point the human brain changes from a sponge to a sieve."

"I don't think *I'll* get any worse," AJ said.

"I agree. You couldn't possibly get any worse."

"You would know!" AJ laughed.

Some days have themes. Today was one of them, the theme of easy-goingness and its opposite recurring yet again in an afternoon encounter with Ben Bruce. I was behind the wheel of the Fun Mobile, on my way back to Matt's place from Fort Tuthill Park after my afternoon run, when I saw Ben loping gracefully along the sidewalk in the same direction. I was just about to tap the horn when a mischievous impulse stayed my hand, and instead I hit the gas, shooting past him with a scheme forming in my head.

By the time Ben reached the point where Matt's street branches off the main road, I was standing directly in his path, proffering an unopened bottle of Breckenridge Brewery Oatmeal Stout that Josh Bolton had left behind when he and Tanis returned to Toronto a couple of days ago. An amused smile creased Ben's face as he approached, but instead of waving away the gag gift and running on by, as I'd pictured him doing, he stopped and took the beverage from me.

"You want me to carry this all the way back to my house?" he said, noting the bottle's unopened state.

"I didn't really think it through," I confessed. "I suppose that probably wouldn't turn out very well."

"It's nice and cold, too. Is it a twist-off?"

"No, it's not," I said, deflated. "To be honest, I wasn't expecting you to take it."

"I totally would have split it with you."

"What can I say?" I said, lowering my eyes. "I underestimated you."

Ben ran on and I toddled back to the house, wondering if I might have been a better runner if I were less high-strung.

29 Days to Chicago

Hearing the telltale sounds of Matt's breakfast preparations in the kitchen (it's hard to miss the assaultive whir of a Vitamix), I tossed aside the heating pad that had been wrapped around my upper left thigh for the past eight minutes and raced downstairs.

"Are you ready for my Question of the Day?" I asked

"Something tells me I'm going to hear it regardless," he laughed.

Question of the Day has become an inside joke between us over the past nine weeks, a playful acknowledgment of the full advantage I've taken of living under the same roof as a real pro runner with an eminently pickable brain. Taking his response as a "yes," I fired away.

"Do you have any advice you can give me on choosing bottles for the Chicago Marathon?"

One of the perks of racing as an elite is access to elite fluid stations—tables positioned at five-kilometer intervals where runners with two-digit bib numbers are able to snatch their own personal bottles containing whatever they please. With less than a month left before the event, I'm feeling pressed to figure out what I'm going to use so I can practice with it.

"It's really a matter of personal preference," Matt said, abandoning his breakfast preparations and opening up a cupboard that was filled with plastic bottles of every description. "I used these at the Olympic Trials, and I might use them again in Frankfurt."

He pulled out a bright blue one with the number 3 scrawled on one side in indelible ink and handed it to me.

"What do you like about them?" I asked, studying it.

"I like that they cost a dollar."

I laughed. Matt didn't.

"Seriously," he said. "You don't get your bottles back from the race organizer. If you spend ten bucks per bottle for eight bottles, that's a lot of money for something you use once."

"I heard the organizers supply bottles," I said. "That seems like the cheapest way to go."

"They do, but the problem is they all look the same. There are stickers and stuff they give you to decorate them with, but everyone's using the same decorations so it doesn't really work. At the Trials the organizers gave out bottles with the Coca-Cola logo on them because they were a sponsor. I was amazed by how many people used them."

Still acting as though he had nothing better to do today than help me choose bottles for the Chicago Marathon, Matt described the preferences of some other pro runners. Kellyn buys little eight-ounce bottles of juice intended for kids, pours out the juice, and uses the bottles, which she likes because they're small. Dathan Ritzenhein, a three-time Olympian, uses laboratory soap bottles with a rigid straw that allows him to spray the drink into his mouth, which is less disruptive to breathing.

"So, those are some options," he said. "Which way are you leaning?"

"Hot pink," I said. "Since I'll probably be the last runner to reach each table, I want something that no one will grab by mistake."

Grinning, Matt reached into the cupboard again and pulled out a hot-pink bottle with the Hoka brand logo on it.

"Yeah, that's the idea," I said. "But as for the design, I have no clue. I like the idea of small bottles. And spray bottles seem worth a try. I didn't realize what a Pandora's box I was opening."

"In that case, why don't you just use the same thing you used in your last marathon?"

Matt knew perfectly well, of course, that in my last marathon, and in every other marathon I've run, I drank from Dixie cups like any other amateur.

"Touché," I said.

28 Days to Chicago

The workout that Coach Ben had intended to serve as a sort of a dress rehearsal for my fast-approaching marathon—a twelve-mile steady-state run on Lake Mary Road—became a literal dress rehearsal when I chose my clothing this morning. Passing over the musty old shirts and shorts I brought from California, I suited up instead in the skimpy NAZ Elite race uniform that had caused me such discomfiture before the High Street Hustle, plus a fresh-out-of-the-box pair of Hoka Tracers (a gift from Ben Bruce, for whom they're a half size too small) the same ensemble I will wear in Chicago.

It turned out I wasn't alone in my sartorial mindset for the day. As a pale morning sun peeped over the swaying, green steeples of the fir trees ringing Lake Mary Start's dirt parking area, my teammates arrived by ones and twos decked out in their newest, smartest NAZ Elite apparel (everyone, that is, except Aaron, who always just tosses on whatever passes the smell test), Coach Ben having deliberately planned dress-rehearsal workouts of one kind or another for all of the fall marathon runners. Behaving very much like an auteur on the eve of opening night, Ben made the rounds among us, nailing down final logistics. When my turn came, I petitioned him for permission to roll straight from my two-mile warm-up into the steady-state portion of the workout instead of pausing to change shoes and do drills and strides, a deviation from standard procedure that would give me an extra opportunity to work on drinking on the fly. Ben approved the plan, which pleased me, but to execute it I needed one thing more: Eric

Fernandez, whom Ben had recruited to provide drink support but who hadn't been heard from since yesterday.

At 7:05, a lone, straggling vehicle rumbled into the parking area, and my hopes rose, but they fell just as quickly when Kellyn's scowling face appeared behind the windshield. Leaping from her barely stopped truck like an overcaffeinated bull rider, she stomped straight toward Ben with fisted hands.

"This is *way* too early to run," she spat.

Ben merely chuckled. He's well accustomed to Kellyn's withering expressions of displeasure, and this one was no worse than past outbursts, including "This is just stupid" (spoken to Ben when Kellyn arrived at a leg speed workout that was to be done on a snow-covered field) and "Terrible place for a bottle" (spoken to Ben when he handed her a bottle of water on a gnarly hill during a depletion run).

I warmed up alone, running a mile toward town before turning around and retracing my steps. When I came back within sight of Lake Mary Start, where my workout would officially begin, I still saw no sign of my wingman, whom I now pictured in bed, his large body huddled in a fetal curl, sleeping off the hangover he'd earned while watching his beloved Arkansas Razorbacks get pummeled by TCU on the gridiron yesterday. But no sooner had I resigned myself to setting off without a first dose of Maurten than he came bursting out of the woods like a jolly Sasquatch and lumbered across the road, bottle in hand.

"Don't worry, Fitz!" he shouted. "Big Dog's got you covered!"

We converged on the stenciled yellow "S" with balletic timing, as though we'd practiced the maneuver. In a single motion, I took the bottle from Eric (just a regular bottle—I still haven't decided what I'm going to use in Chicago), pressed the lap button on my watch, and accelerated to my target pace of 6:25 per mile, looking forward to the next twelve miles in a way no normal person looks forward to prolonged high-intensity exercise.

From the very first stride I knew my Lake Mary Magic was back. I felt every inch the runner I was in my last big workout there—the one that had been the best run of my life until, in a single, horrible instant, it became the worst.

At four miles, still floating, I came upon Sarah Crouch, who stood in an expectant posture like a relay partner. Instead of receiving a baton from me and blasting off alone, however, Sarah fell in beside me, having proposed the idea of running together at the parking area when we described our respective workouts and discovered a degree of overlap. In due deference to her status as the real pro, I let Sarah control the pace, but she did so rather erratically, I must say, apologizing now and again when a quarter-mile split was particularly far off the mark. Otherwise we spoke little, and in our lengthy shared silences I couldn't help but notice that Sarah's breathing was a bit more labored than mine, and I sensed that she noticed this also. Given our prior trash talk, I was more than a little tempted to rub her face in my apparent advantage, but I held back, knowing she'll probably have the last laugh on October 8.

Midway through my ninth mile, Michael Crouch, now just three weeks out from the Twin Cities Marathon, glided by.

"Looking good, babe," Sarah called out.

Michael was still within sight up the road when Brauny, Ben Bruce, Faubs, and Matt streaked past as though hunting Sarah's husband. It's funny how, after you've spent a little time around a runner, you know exactly how he's feeling on a given day based on cues so subtle they almost defy description. Something in Aaron's bearing—a hint of confidence in his slightly upraised chin? A faint ease in the loose curl of his fingers?—told me he was also enjoying a bit of Lake Mary Magic today.

I took my last bottle at nine miles, Eric running alongside me while I quaffed the whole 8.5 ounces before relieving me of the empty container. I still haven't gotten used to the notion of a 2:14 marathoner playing water boy to a 2:41 marathoner, and at this point, I suppose, I never will.

Sarah peeled off at ten miles. She'd run a bunch of hill repetitions before she joined me and would wrap up her workout with a few more. Continuing alone, I soon caught up to a solitary, jogging Ben Bruce, who shouldn't have been alone or jogging but still burning up the road with his former companions. Something was wrong.

"Are you doing 6:30s?" he asked, adjusting his tempo to match mine.

"Six-twenties," I said, giving him the pace I'd actually been running rather than the pace I was supposed to be. "What are *you* doing?"

"I'm cooling down."

"How did your workout go?" I asked, already knowing the answer.

"Not good. I only made it eight."

"Shit. Sorry."

Without announcing his intention, Ben paced me through the remainder of my eleventh mile. As we passed over the stenciled "11" on the road's shoulder, he slowed to a more appropriate cooldown pace, which frankly wasn't all that much slower than he'd been running with me, and I was on my own again.

"The last quarter's a bitch!" he shouted from behind. "Bank some time!"

Coach Ben and Eric received me with high fives at Mile 12, my finish line for the day. After cooling down, I jumped into the back of Sarah Cotton's Jeep with Michael and Futsum for the return trip to Lake Mary Start, which somehow seemed immeasurably farther on wheels than it had on foot. Along the way, Sarah received a call from Coach Ben with the news that a serious accident had occurred at Mile 3. Minutes later, we came upon a mangled Harley-Davidson lying like a slaughtered horse in the southbound lane, surrounded by flashing emergency vehicles.

Back at the parking area, we got the full story from Ben Bruce and Big Dog, who'd had the unenviable experience of witnessing the crash. Evidently, the pair had been on their way back to Lake Mary Start when they stopped to hand a drink bottle to Kellyn. As they awaited her approach, a half-ton elk bolted from the trees, heading straight for the road. At the same moment, a motorcycle crested a hill just ahead. Ben and Eric could only watch in helpless horror as the oblivious elk T-boned the bike at full gallop, sending the machine and its two occupants skidding across the tarmac. Unfazed, Bullwinkle charged on. Profoundly fazed, Ben sprinted toward the victims.

"The woman sat up right away," he told us, "but the man was motionless. I swear to God, I thought he was dead." While Ben attended to the victims, Eric called 9-1-1. On reaching the scene, Kellyn interrupted her workout to see if her recently acquired paramedic skills were needed, but she quickly resumed at Ben's insistence. At last the man began to stir, his agonized groans launching the woman into hysterics. An ambulance arrived, and then a fire truck, and then a police car, and at that point Ben and Eric recognized the redundancy of their presence and split.

Both men were still plainly rattled, their voices tight, pupils like marbles, but it was Ben especially that my heart went out to. He turned thirty-five years old today. I rather doubt he's had many worse birthdays.

26 Days to Chicago

Ben Bruce was conspicuously absent at Walnut Canyon this morning. Eager for news about him, I collared Steph while she performed one of her signature pre-run muscle activation exercises. (Picture a person in a full-body cast attempting to touch her toes from a standing position: ankles crossed, arms extended downward, she reached her left hand toward the left foot, then her right hand toward the right foot, with zero bending at the knees or hips but only a slight side-to-side compression of the spine.)

"How's your better half?" I asked.

"He's okay," Steph sighed. "He's just taking a break."

She told me how the rest of his birthday had gone. After returning home from his disastrous workout and the elk–motorcycle incident, Ben received a text from Coach Ben summoning him to The Coffee Bean, where the leader of NAZ Elite was holed up for the afternoon writing training plans. When Ben got there, his coach told him what he knew already—that a fall marathon was now out of the question and he would need to take some time off and let his abdominal strain heal fully. Ben put up no resistance. As much as he hated to admit it, he knew it was the right call.

"The last thing you want to do is waste a marathon," Coach Ben said. *Especially at your age*, he might have added.

Head swimming, Ben left the coffee shop and drove around aimlessly, returning at one point to the site of the workout that had put a final nail in the coffin of his fall marathon plans—and possibly in his professional running career. When he came home again, he went straight to his and Steph's bedroom and shut the door.

"Not much of a celebration," I said.

"No," Steph agreed. "I baked him a cake, and he didn't even touch it. But he'll bounce back quickly; he always does."

We took the usual route, heading east on Old Walnut Canyon Road for a short distance before picking up the Campbell Mesa Loop. The team soon separated along gender lines—Kellyn, Rochelle, and Steph sticking together as Aaron, Craig, Faubs, Futsum, Matt, and Scott Smith eased ahead. Only when the gals had drifted out of earshot did I realize that, for once, I was up with the guys.

Loping along at the rear of the line, basking in the empyrean warmth of a slanting mid-September sunlight, I wondered how this was going to work. Everyone else was running ten miles to my eight. If I turned back alone at four miles, I risked getting lost in the maze of forking paths that everyone except me seemed to know like New York City taxi drivers know Manhattan. But if I stayed with the big boys I risked running two extra miles. After weighing both options, I decided to just go with the flow and see what happened.

The group was curiously hushed. Except for a brief conversation about beer ("I drink Budweiser almost exclusively when I'm in LA because I can't afford to drink anything else," Scott Smith remarked from the front), little was said in the first couple of miles. If I didn't know any better, I might have assumed these people did not enjoy one another's company—or enjoy running, for that matter. Having been among them for more than nine weeks, however, I figured everyone was just plain tired, subdued by a full summer of triple-digit-mileage weeks and huge workouts (which would also explain why I was keeping up with them).

"How's this pace for you, Fitz?" Futsum asked from his position directly in front of me, as though reading my thoughts.

"It's fine," I said. "I had a day off yesterday."

"It's kicking my ass," Futsum said.

Minutes later, Faubs suddenly dropped back from the head of the line and took my place at the rear. I asked him if he was having a rough day, too.

"No, I've just been voted off the front," he said.

"Why? What did you do?"

"Crop dusted," Faubs said with a hint of pride.

All runners pass gas while running, but not all runners have a reputation for doing so. Matt blames Fauble's flatulence on excessive burrito consumption, but as far as I know, he doesn't eat burritos for breakfast, so maybe it's just a minor issue with his plumbing.

"Tell me something," I said, as though changing the subject. "Do you really love burritos as much as you say?"

According to his Twitter profile, Faubs is "constantly searching for the perfect burrito." A plurality of his tweets are burrito-related.

"I do believe that burritos are very good," he said judiciously. "The best, actually. But I don't think any person could love anything as much as I claim to love burritos on Twitter."

"How did the whole thing get started anyway?"

"It started in college. My friends and I used to go to this place in Portland called Boulevard Tacos every Friday. I started tweeting 'Just got a burrito!' or 'Eating a burrito!' every time I went to Boulevard, just as way to make fun of people's lame attempts at using social media to report on mundane things. Coincidentally, or maybe not, I began picking up followers through running at about the same time I was tweeting a lot about burritos, and so, naturally, the increased followers reinforced my behavior. And now it's cyclical: I tweet about burritos and get likes and follows, so I have to continue to tweet about burritos in order to keep those followers, and myself, happy."

MATT FITZGERALD

A little farther along the trail we stopped to pee.

"I can't believe we haven't even gone five miles," Matt complained, checking his watch as he watered a tree.

"It's weird," said Brauny after we'd gotten moving again. "The faster my workouts get, the slower my easy runs are. I can't wait to see what my workouts look like when I'm doing my easy runs at nine-minute pace."

Having gone way past the midpoint of my run without turning back, I was fully resigned to running the full ten miles with the others when we came to a split in the trail and Brauny pointed right while veering left.

"If you're running eight, you'll want to go that way," he said.

I thanked Aaron for the tip and branched off alone, suddenly disappointed, realizing only then that I had actually *wanted* to finish with my teammates—that, in fact, there was nothing I'd rather do with the next thirty minutes of my life than tag along with a half dozen of the finest distance runners in America, whom I now count as friends, on an leisurely jog along a peaceful mountain trail in the precise weather conditions I would choose if I had twenty-four hours to live and God let me have any weather I liked for this one day.

25 Days to Chicago

Futsum strolled across the gravel parking lot at Buffalo Park with the affected indolence of a high-school student slow-walking toward his least favorite class. On reaching the pagoda underneath which Craig and I awaited him, he addressed me singly, ignoring his fellow real pro.

"I think you're going to like the place, man," he said. "It's the real stuff—the food we eat back home."

"First Cup," I explained to a bemused Craig. "It's an Ethiopian restaurant in Phoenix. I'm going down there on Friday to see John Ball and figured I'd take Nataki with me and have a Date Night."

It was a plan more than two months in the making, originating in Scott Fauble's suggestion during my second week here that I seek out John's services for my ailing left Achilles, services so much in demand that only now was I able to get in. The Ethiopian dinner part was added yesterday, when I visited AJ's office for a checkup on my groin, a visit I dreaded not for the usual reason (pain) but because I felt obligated to inform AJ of my appointment with John, a man who practices the same art (chiropractic, officially) on the same clientele (high-level athletes, mainly runners), but whose reputation, fairly or not, outstrips AJ's by about the same degree that Bob Dylan's did Arlo Guthrie's circa 1968.

"So, I need another restaurant recommendation," I said to him fake-casually while aiming the cold laser at a patch of skin that has become discolored—perhaps permanently—from so much lasering. "Nataki and I are heading to the Valley two days from now. You haven't failed me yet—where should we eat?"

"Are you going to see John?" AJ asked.

My face turned the same color as my overlasered groin. The whole point of asking AJ for a restaurant recommendation in Phoenix was to soften the ground for breaking the news about my chiropractic infidelity. But he'd caught me on my back foot, cutting to the chase with a directness I hadn't anticipated.

"Yes," I confessed.

AJ waved away my embarrassment and told me that when he's in Phoenix he usually eats Ethiopian food, though it's been a while. I asked him if he remembered the name of the place he liked and he told me he went to various places, whichever one was nearest to where he happened to be at the time, and he hadn't been disappointed.

"We'll do the same, then," I said. "That way the trip won't be a complete waste of time, considering I'm not even injured anymore."

"Oh, John will find something to fix," AJ said with a twinkle in his eye. "He always does."

In the evening, when I came downstairs to grab an icepack for my groin, I found Matt bent over the stove stirring a simmering pot of ugali with surgical concentration, having learned how to make the Kenyan national dish (a thick cornmeal paste usually served with stews) from Sally Kipyego and her husband, Kevin Chelimo, when they stayed with him. A conversation about East African cuisine ensued, in the course of which I brought up my intention to grab some Ethiopian grub in Phoenix, and Matt cited Futsum's expertise on the subject.

"He's Eritrean, of course, but it's the same food," he said.

"Yes, I know," I said, as if he'd told me Canada isn't a state.

Craig and Futsum had a short fartlek run plus strides on their schedule—a light workout to prime their legs for Saturday's Cow Harbor 10K, a venerable road race held on Long Island—whereas I had an easy run. Despite our disparate training agendas, Coach Ben had thrown the three of us together so I'd at least have some company for the first three miles of my eight, during the real pros' warm-up.

They started slowly, perhaps for my sake, perhaps not, but in any case I took advantage of the opportunity to pepper my companions with questions about their race. Craig had plenty to say, having studied the course profile (big hill at 1.8 miles) and the list of elite entrants (Don Cabral and Tim Ritchie would be tough to beat). Futsum, more of a show-up-and-run kind of guy, had clearly done neither, but he knew exactly how much dough he would take home if he won: $3,000.

"That's rent money," he said.

This wasn't a figure of speech. Futsum was born in 1992, one year after his homeland, one of the poorest countries in Africa, achieved independence from Ethiopia following a bloody thirty-year civil war. When he was barely a teenager, he spent a year in a refugee camp before emigrating to the US with his parents and seven siblings. Now twenty-four years old and less than one year out of college, Futsum has not only himself to support but a wife, Samra, as well. Having attended the team's new contract meeting a few weeks back, I've got a pretty good idea how much NAZ Elite pays Futsum. If he finishes in the money Saturday, he probably will use it for rent.

"I wish I were going with you guys," I told them. "I will never again be as fit as I am now, and it kills me that it's all for one race."

"Why do you say that?" Futsum asked.

"Because I'm forty-six years old!" I said. "And in four weeks I'll be back home, at sea level, training on boring farm roads without a coach or you guys or Hypo2."

When Futsum came to America in 2008, he spoke little English. Outgoing by nature, he became withdrawn in Indianapolis, unable to find his place. It was running that turned things around for him. Under the mentorship of Central High School coach Rick Stover, Futsum blossomed into a state and national champion and earned a full scholarship at NAU, becoming a fully assimilated American along the way. He still holds back around new people, as indeed he did with me before today, but when he's given an opening (such as a request to recommend an Ethiopian restaurant in Phoenix), his full personality emerges. Suddenly interested in me, he turned the tables and quizzed me through the remainder of the warm-up. On learning that I've run more than forty marathons, he just about fell over, uttering a sobriquet that I fear might become his nickname for me: "Crazy Man."

"Let me know how you like First Cup," he said to me later, back at the parking lot, after we'd completed our respective sessions. "And remember to tell them Futsum sent you."

23 Days to Chicago

I was staring at a muscle chart on a wall inside a generic-looking physical therapy treatment room when a man burst through the door and quickly shut it behind him, pressing his back to it as though escaping some untoward occurrence outside.

It was John Ball in the flesh, looking nothing like I'd pictured him. He wore knee-length shorts, fashion sneakers, and a T-shirt with the name of his clinic silkscreened across the chest. A mop of chestnut curls perched insouciantly atop his head. He could almost have passed for a prep school lacrosse player.

"So, you're the writer," he said, plopping himself down on a stool at the foot of the table and placing a small notepad in front of him.

When I reached out to John's scheduler nine weeks ago, I used every trick I could think of to jump the waitlist and score an immediate appointment, including dropping Matt Llano's name and, yes, hinting that John's expeditious treatment of my Achilles injury would be rewarded with immortalization in a book about my experience as a fake pro runner. None of it had worked, but I held no grudge, and here we were now chatting chummily about my time with NAZ Elite and how it had affected my body—so chummily, in fact, that I was beginning to doubt the various descriptions I'd heard of John as arrogant, condescending, and mean, when he abruptly cut me off midsentence and ordered me to remove my shoes and socks.

I shut up and bared my feet. John then began to study my lower extremities with his hands, doing so in the tender, searching way of a blind man learning a new face. As his fingers poked and prodded, his lips issued a steady stream of hushed, almost whispered questions and commands. *Turn onto your stomach . . . Press against my hand with your foot . . . Does this hurt?* Seldom was I able to say more than a few words in answer to one question before John broke in with another, like Chris Matthews interviewing a guest on his cable news show, able apparently to judge from eight or ten syllables out of my mouth whether he'd hit a dead end or found a lead worth pursuing.

The whole situation was just beginning to feel a little less weird when John leapt up from the stool and waved me into the facility's large, high-ceilinged main room, which was empty save for a wall-facing treadmill in one corner, a second treatment table in another, and a few other appurtenances of the trade scattered here and there.

"Kyle!" he shouted into the empty space as I followed John toward the back.

An athletic-looking fellow of about John's age dutifully appeared. At his boss's behest, he assumed a crouching position beside him against the room's far wall. I was instructed now to walk back and forth barefoot from one end of the space to the other as the two colleagues studied my movements, pointing things out to each other and speaking in low voices. I felt like a 400-pound acne sufferer auditioning for a fitness modeling gig—so self-conscious I could scarcely keep my balance.

"Did you bring running shoes?" John asked me after four or five laps. "Good. Hop on the treadmill over there."

I began jogging and John and Kyle continued their inspection from a position directly behind me. At the risk of flying off the back of the machine, I craned my neck at one point to see how my performance was being judged and caught John imitating my simian walking style, evidently explaining to Kyle some abnormality of my gait pattern. His intentions were purely clinical—I understood this—but the behavior looked (and felt) like straight-up schoolyard mockery.

It was with great but shortsighted relief that I was led next from the treadmill back to the treatment table, where John set to work on my left foot and ankle, manipulating these parts of my anatomy like a sculptor struggling to reshape a piece of clay that had come out all wrong on the first try, except that my foot was not made of clay but of living flesh, and his molding efforts hurt like a motherfucker (to use Faubs's words). As before, John kept up a steady patter while he worked, asking me how this or that felt, sharing his observations, and thinking out loud, all in the same barely audible undertone. Earlier I had dismissed John's murmuring as an affectation, a cultivated part of his savant act, but the longer he went on without breaking character, the more convinced I became that the savant act was in fact the real John Ball. What I couldn't figure out, despite the voluminous output of words, was what the hell he was trying to accomplish.

"I'm looking for the best way to attack this," he said in answer to my thoughts.

"Attack what?" I asked.

Seeming to ignoring the question, John offered a demonstration, twisting my right foot as far as it would go in either direction—toes out, toes in—and then doing the same with my left foot, which had a much more limited range of motion, something I had never noticed.

"There are only so many structures in the foot," he explained, "that could be responsible for this kind of restriction."

John then proceeded to dig his fingers into the outer part of the ankle. I felt no pain, and it was clear that John had expected none.

"It's not this," he said.

Repositioning his fingers at the back of the ankle, John dug in again. Still no pain.

"And it's not this."

By this point I had a pretty good idea what was coming. John dug his fingers into the medial side of the ankle, my reaction to which was a hissing intake of breath. *It's this.*

"But what has that got to do with my Achilles tendon?" I asked.

John answered with another demonstration. He rolled my foot inward and punched the sole with the side of his fist. I felt my lower leg absorb the impact nicely. Flattening my foot, John punched again. This time I felt the impact all the way up to my knee. John explained that when the foot *everts*, or rolls inward, as it is supposed to during running, the big toe lines up with the heel and the heel with the leg, a "stacking" of the kinetic chain that is very stable and minimizes stress to the bones and soft tissues. When the foot is restricted and does not evert as it should, like mine, other structures that are not designed for stabilizing have to pitch in and take up the big toe's slack, causing damage that, with enough repetition, may eventually become an outright breakdown.

"And the Achilles is one of those structures," I said.

"Actually, no," John said. "You don't have an Achilles injury—at least not mainly."

I eyed him askance, dubious. Unbothered, John pinched a spot on the back of my lower leg between his thumb and index finger.

"Does that hurt?" he asked.

"Not much," I said.

"That's your Achilles," he said.

John moved his digits a tiny bit lower and gave me another pinch.

"YOU FUCKER!" I shouted, quoting without intent from the famous chest-hair-waxing scene in *The 40-Year-Old Virgin*.

"That's the insertion point of the plantaris muscle," John whispered, "which *does* jump in to help stabilize in certain circumstances. And another one is the anterior femoral ligament."

John reached all the way up to my knee and poked a finger into a spot on the outside of the joint. My body shot off the table as though electrocuted.

"How did you know?" I asked.

"Lucky guess," he shrugged.

I remained in the office two more hours, learning a few new rehab exercises from another of John's colleagues, Boone, a strength and conditioning specialist, and grimacing through a second round of foot remolding. Worried that I might have fallen victim to torturing kidnappers, Nataki, who'd been waiting for me outside in the Fun Mobile, wandered into the building around 1:30 in the afternoon (we'd arrived at 11:30 in the morning) to find John Ball gripping my left shin and forcibly bending the knee in an effort to restore the 15 degrees of motion range I lost after ACL surgery thirty-two years ago, a tableau that, judging by the look on her face, confirmed that I had indeed fallen into the hands of torturing kidnappers.

It was pushing 2:30 when I was at last released. On my way out, I stopped by the reception desk to fork over $391 and make two more appointments with John Ball in the next two weeks, the latest convert.

20 Days to Chicago

Soldiers. That's what my teammates reminded me of this morning as we mustered outside Coach Ben's house for another Monday easy run. A platoon of weary and bedraggled infantrymen and -women gearing up for a long hump in the middle of a bloody campaign inside enemy territory.

Faubs's eyes were slits. Steph couldn't stop yawning. Brauny's hairline seemed to have receded since yesterday.

My mind went back to the very first Monday run I did with the team, ten weeks ago. Most of the runners were fresh off a spring break then, recharged, good-humored, and excited for their fall races. Having just met them, I assumed they were always like this. How naïve I was! Now everyone is in survival mode, looking as though they've just woken up, no matter the time of day. Coach Ben says there comes a point in each training segment when he looks at his athletes and thinks, *What the hell am I doing to these people?* I imagined him having this very thought when he stepped out his front door to join us and saw what I was seeing.

We started with palpable reluctance, like so many swimmers plunging into a cold pool at dawn. Within half a mile or so the customary gender split had occurred and I found myself back in the familiar company of Kellyn, Rochelle, and Steph.

"Well, it's just us ladies now," I joked.

"Oh, stop!" Steph laughed.

Kellyn threw a couple of quick sideways glances my way, as if noticing me for the first time, or else saying to herself, *Wait,* you're *still here?*

"What's your goal for Chicago?" she asked.

"It's been kind of a moving target," I said, realizing this was the first question Kellyn had ever asked me. "I've never trained at altitude before. My workouts have gone really well for the most part, but I have a hard time convincing myself I can run twenty seconds per mile faster at sea level."

"Me, too," Kellyn said. "That's why I like to run the marathon-pace stuff at lower elevation. Then I know for sure."

"Well, I get to run in Camp Verde on Wednesday," I said, referring to a town thirty miles south of Flagstaff that serves as the primary location for NAZ Elite's lower-elevation workouts. "Maybe I'll gain some confidence there."

"You haven't answered my question," Kellyn said.

"Two thirty-nine."

We caught up to the guys where the Arizona Trail branches off Mt. Elden Lookout Road, their chosen location for a pit stop. From there the reconstituted group proceeded two by two along the trail, Kellyn remaining beside me at the rear of the procession. Gesturing toward the virgin forest around us, she told me it would soon be transformed into new housing developments. Her remark had the tone of a complaint, and thus it was in the tone of apology that I confessed Nataki and I have been looking at local real estate—new construction specifically.

"So, you guys are thinking about staying here?" she asked.

"Thinking about it," I said.

The notion of moving to Flagstaff, or at least purchasing a second home here, first came up between Nataki and me several weeks ago, when I put out a very carefully worded feeler, something like, "Could you imagine yourself ever living in a place like this?" I certainly could. If you ask me, Flagstaff has it all: Spectacular natural beauty crowned by the most stunning night sky I've ever seen? Check. A thousand and one great places to run? Check. Good food, great coffee, and (thanks to the presence of a major university) a left-leaning political atmosphere and a bit of culture? Check, check, and check.

But Flagstaff's greatest attraction for me is the people. Not since college have I found myself in a place where I've made so many friends so quickly. Big Dog, Too Slow, Sarah Crouch, James McKirdy (who, though back home in Connecticut now, has been making noise about moving here with Heather Szuba), Coach Ben, Matt—these are folks I want to keep in my life. In Flagstaff I feel part of a community, whereas at home in California Nataki and I live in relative isolation, many miles from our nearest close friends. As a self-employed writer, I can live anywhere. So, the real question, I've begun to think, is not "Why move to Flagstaff?" but "Why not?"

A week ago today Nataki and I toured Pine Canyon, a swanky new golf community I pass by each time I run at either Woody Mountain Road (left at the T-junction) or Kiltie Loop (right). Aloof at first, our guide warmed up to us increasingly as we zoomed around the property in a golf cart and Nataki and I demonstrated a perhaps unexpected level of seriousness as prospective buyers by pricing out specific builds on specific available lots and gushing over the posh clubhouse, the views of the San Francisco peaks, and the multimillion-dollar homes that command these views. Despite having come with some reluctance, Nataki got caught up in the fantasy no less than I, asking our guide how bad the winters in Flagstaff are, whether residents are allowed to install solar panels on their homes, and what buyers get for the mandatory $30,000 social membership fee.

We left with a brochure and a business card and visions of a new life in one of Flagstaff's most exclusive neighborhoods. But the spell broke on the drive back to Matt's house, and I began to have second thoughts. All of a sudden our Pine Canyon visit seemed wrong, or if not wrong, forced. I saw my flirtation with relocating to Flagstaff from a different perspective, not as a sensible way to create a better match between my lifestyle and my environment but as a desperate attempt to prolong an experience whose preciousness, like that of life itself, is inseparable from its brevity.

Thirteen weeks of living a dream and then back to reality—that was the plan. The first ten weeks have been truly dreamlike, but isn't this partly because each passing day subtracts one from an inflexible total? After a full year here, two years, three, what would my life be—a dream still or a pitiful backward-looking wakefulness?

"What about you?" I asked Kellyn. "Do you think you'll stay in Flag after you retire from racing?"

"I doubt it. We'll probably want to move closer to Kylyn's grandparents. She has one set in Kansas and another in Wisconsin."

"I get it," I said. "My mom was recently diagnosed with Alzheimer's and it's made me feel differently about living so far from her and my dad."

"That's a weird disease," Kellyn said without emotion. "Very strange."

I sensed she was thinking of someone in particular, and I had just opened my mouth to ask if Alzheimer's ran in her family when we were separated by a moment of chaos caused by a missed turn, and that was the end of that.

After the run, Craig and I sat together on the back bumper of the Fun Mobile for a few minutes and chatted about Wednesday's trip down to Camp Verde.

"What's your workout?" I asked.

"Three-mile tempo at four fifty-seven pace, three times a mile in four forty, four thirty-six, and four thirty-two, three-mile tempo at four fifty-two pace,' he rattled off.

"That's exactly what I'm doing!" I said.

Craig threw me a doubtful look.

"Except with fives instead of fours," I added.

18 Days to Chicago

Camp Verde is a mostly empty expanse of high desert country whose chief virtue (as far as outsiders are concerned, anyway) is that it's a convenient place to buy gas if you're traveling between Flagstaff and Phoenix. In the southern part of its forty-two square miles sits an area of modest homes in various states of disrepair separated by broad fields gone to weeds. At seven o'clock this morning, Coach Ben parked the Pilot on a dead-end spur jutting off the neighborhood's narrow main road, I parked the Fun Mobile directly behind him, and the NAZ Elite crew spilled out into a palpably denser atmosphere than the one we'd recently left, the runners among us immediately setting about shaking the travel from our legs.

Throughout the ensuing warm-up, as the only first-time visitor in the group, I studied the surroundings with touristic interest while the others focused on the ground in front of them. In the early going we passed a small sign half hidden in dry brush on the west side of the street, marking an otherwise unremarkable ditch. "Historical Camp Verde—Diamond S Ditch—1892," it read.

"What is Camp Verde known for?" I asked.

"Crystal meth, mostly," Craig said.

On our way back to the cars, I spotted a couple of hairy piglike critters bounding through the front yards of the homes to our right, intermittently disappearing behind vegetation and then reappearing. Craig was next to notice them.

"Check it out!" he exclaimed. "Are those javelina?"

"I think so," Aaron said.

"*Yes!*" Craig exulted, pumping his fist like a golfer who's just chipped in for birdie.

"Is that a good omen?" I asked.

"Two javelinas before workout at Camp Verde very good sign," Craig intoned in the voice of a Hollywood Indian chief. "Means you will run like fat little piggy."

"This little piggy ran four fifty-seven pace," Brauny said.

Milking the theme, we began naming animals that by rights shouldn't be able to outsprint humans but can (crocodiles, kangaroos, ostriches). Aaron wondered aloud how much faster humans could run if we had tails.

After drills and strides, Coach Ben chauffeured us over to the starting point of the three-part workout, a three-mile tempo. Batting leadoff as always, I walked alone to the first cone and crouched in the ready position, eyes on the road ahead, where several mangy dogs snooped at the edges, noses to the ground.

"I feel like a sacrifice," I said.

Coach Ben assured me the dogs were harmless, then reminded me to stick to my prescribed pace of 6:00 per mile.

"It's time to get serious," he said. "You're running out of chances to dial in your marathon pace."

I had every intention of being compliant. But I was at 3,100 feet, where a 6:00 mile feels like a 6:15 mile to someone who's spent the last ten and a half weeks at 7,000 feet. And so it was that I completed the first mile in 5:54, at which point, feeling too damn good to slow down, I decided to just go with the flow, the result of which was back-to-back 5:51s. Aaron, Craig, and Futsum finished right behind me, having nailed their (this little piggy ran) 4:57 splits perfectly.

We slurped from our drink bottles and then jogged together to the starting point of part two, Futsum asking us along the way what was next, because he had no idea. With a defeated head shake, Craig filled him in: three times one mile on two minutes' rest, cutting down from 4:40.

"Don't get pulled along by these guys," Coach Ben instructed me as I took a deferential position behind my teammates at the cone. Then, to the entire group: "Okay, everyone ready?"

"Hold on, Coach," Futsum said, raising an index finger.

"What is it?" Ben asked.

"Hold on," Futsum repeated.

A shrill squeaking sound, like a balloon losing air, issued from someplace other than Futsum's mouth.

"Okay," he said.

What can I say? I did get pulled along, my teammates' flawlessly paced 4:40 mile towing me to a 5:32, eight seconds too fast. I took another swig of Maurten, caught my breath, and lined up to run back in the other direction.

"Keep it right there," Ben said.

Meaning: *Don't you dare run any faster on this next one.* But I just *had to* run faster, and so I did, by three seconds, finishing as the others, who had hit their target time of 4:36 on the nose, launched into their third and final rep, acknowledging me with collegial head nods.

Again Coach Ben warned me not to run any faster, and again I disobeyed, clocking an errant 5:27 to the bull's eye 4:32 recorded by the big boys, who, despite my overzealous pacing, were already out of sight up the road when I started part three, another three-mile tempo. The real pros were supposed to run 4:52s, and did. I was supposed to run 5:55s, but instead logged splits of 5:50, 5:46, and 5:43.

Coach Ben, Brauny, Craig, Futsum, and Sarah Cotton stood waiting at the finish cone as I made my final approach. Craig put his hands together and the others followed suit, clapping and shouting, "Go, Fitz!" and, "Come on, Matt!"

Before I came to Flagstaff, I tried to imagine what it would be like to train with world-class runners day in and day out. I kept picturing myself straggling to the finish of the last repetition of a hard workout and receiving a pity clap from my teammates—the kind of clap a football player gets when he's carried off the field on a cart. The waning moments of today's workout matched this vision in almost every detail. Except I heard no pity in the sounds my teammates made for me.

14 Days to Chicago

Autumn has come to Flagstaff. I left Matt's house this morning swaddled against a forty-degree chill in my warmest warm-ups, and even went so far as to activate the Fun Mobile's heated seats for the first time since March on the short drive to Lake Mary Start, my fake pro runner theme song serving as much to stimulate heat-generating body movement as to psych me up for my last big test before Chicago: twelve miles at marathon effort followed by a three-mile cutdown.

Everybody feeling something
We got the place erupting, erupting

I was feeling something, alright. But it wasn't just the usual adrenaline surge. It was also a pang of anticipatory nostalgia, as though I were listening to a song I associated with a happy time long past.

In my eagerness for the workout, I mistimed my departure, arriving at my destination to the anticlimactic welcome of a deserted parking lot. Coach Ben showed up next, looking as fired up as I felt.

"I tell you, this never gets old," he said by way of greeting, hands wrapped around a steaming cup of coffee.

Just then a familiar truck rumbled in, a little too fast, stopping hard beside the Fun Mobile. The driver door flew open and Kellyn leapt out like a first responder arriving at a disaster scene, slammed the door shut, and stormed toward Coach Ben.

"How fast are the surges?" Kellyn demanded.

She and Steph were scheduled to run twenty miles, alternating between marathon effort and easy pace, with a few surprise surges thrown at them by Big Dog to simulate the tactical racing style that typically plays out at the New York City Marathon.

"I can't tell you," Ben said patiently.

"That's *not* very realistic!"

Ben gave me a sly wink, beaming.

I warmed up with Brauny, Craig, Kellyn, Steph, and Too Slow. Three right turns brought us to Ranch Road, an unpaved sylvan lane that dead-ends just past Kellyn's house. Somehow or another we got onto the topic of music, each of us taking an informal turn to share what we've been listening to lately. When my turn came, I mentioned not only Marlon Roudette but also the fact that Coach Ben had given me permission to wear earbuds during my workout.

"Really?" Steph said with a hint of judgment. "Are you going to listen to music in Chicago?"

"Of course not," I said. "I'm racing as an elite—it's against the rules."

"That's interesting," Steph said.

"Oh, come on, Steph!" I protested. "Let a man have a little distraction. Unlike *you*, I have to do my workout alone."

"I just find that music changes my whole perception of effort," Steph said.

"Exactly!" I countered. "And so does having someone to run with!"

"I think people should do whatever works for them," Kellyn said.

"*Thank you*, Kellyn," I said pointedly, as if switching allegiances.

As it turned out, I did not have to do my workout entirely alone. Bob, who's also running New York, was doing the same workout as Kellyn and Steph only slower, and it so happened that the pace Coach Ben had given him for his fast miles, 6:30, was close enough to my target pace of 6:20 that we agreed to meet in the middle and enjoy one mile of each other's company before splitting up to wage our separate battles. Once again, I knew from the very first step that I was going to have my best legs today—one last dose of Lake Mary Magic. We hit the one-mile mark at 6:20 on the dot, at which point Too Slow wished me well and backed off, and I cued up my playlist.

At three miles, I took a drink bottle from Coach Ben, a royal blue twenty-ounce screw-top with the Hoka logo on it, the very type I've chosen for Chicago, not because it's perfect but because my long search for the perfect bottle led me to conclude that pretty much any bottle will do—and because Ben has boxes of them at his house.

Approaching four miles, I saw Rochelle standing expectantly at the edge of the road, and for a dreadful instant I feared she was going to reprise the infamous cooldown incident that occurred between us at Kiltie Loop a couple of weeks back. To my great relief, however, she merely clapped and told me I looked good (whether she believed it or not) as I passed.

Between five and six miles, Aaron and Craig caught me, Craig raising a hand to invite a high five as the duo slid by, and I knew he must have good legs, too.

At twelve miles, I took my last bottle from Coach Ben and started the cutdown, the rules of which required that I run each remaining mile faster than the one before, but without exceeding a "speed limit" of 5:55. My plan was to game the system and run the three miles in 5:57, 5:56, and 5:55, in part because I knew I could and in part to prove a point to Ben, who, I was keenly aware, would base my official Chicago Marathon target pace on how I performed today.

I completed Mile 13 in 5:56 (close enough), then increased my effort another smidge. Lacking Ben Bruce's eidetic knowledge of Lake Mary Road's topography, I discovered only as I made my way through Mile 14 that it's mostly downhill, and the combination of gravity's friendly assist and that extra soupçon of effort resulted in a split of 5:45, which left me in a pickle. Already I had broken the speed limit. Should I still respect the rule requiring me to run each mile faster than the one before?

No sooner had I decided to go for broke than the road bent upward and the landscape became more exposed, subjecting my kitelike physique to a stiff headwind. Annoyance prodded me to push even harder. Coach Ben came into view, and my mind flashed back to August 16, when at almost this very spot a white-hot blast of pain brought the best workout I'd ever done to a sudden stop within sight of the end. A superstitious dread flooded through me. *I should slow down,* I thought. Instead, I pushed harder still.

"Five thirty-seven, five thirty-eight," Ben read off his watch as I bore down on him. "Five thirty-nine, five-forty—hey, where are you going?"

I charged past my coach without slowing, much less stopping. Raising a finger to signal "give me a minute," I ran on until my watch beeped, having covered perhaps another forty meters.

"My watched disagreed with your road markings," I explained after walking back to where I was supposed to have stopped.

"You're a piece of work," Ben laughed.

In the happy afterglow of my successful workout I forgot to cool down. Giddy with relief for having arrived at the threshold of my two-week pre-race taper in one piece, I just stood around yakking until reminded that, in fact, I was still two miles short of this threshold. More amused than embarrassed, I jogged back the way I'd come, Ben picking me up fifteen minutes later in a big Mazda SUV he'd borrowed from James McKirdy and Heather Szuba, who made a surprise return to Flagstaff yesterday to hunt for an apartment. Seated in back were Brauny and Craig, who had completed steady states of fourteen and twelve miles, respectively. I could tell from the satisfied look on Aaron's face that he'd had a good day, too, but I asked anyway.

"Oh, yeah," he said. "It was pretty easy, actually."

Coming from him, those words were more or less the equivalent of Mike Tyson's "I'm gonna eat your children."

Once again, the inbound ride to Lake Mary Start seemed a greater distance than the outbound run. Along the way, Coach Ben spotted Rochelle, who had run the last part of Kellyn and Steph's session with them (which explained why I'd seen her waiting expectantly at the side of the road) and was wrapping up her cooldown. Coach Ben pulled over and hopped out to check in with her.

"What was your last mile?" we heard him ask.

"Five thirty-two," she said. "A little slow."

Kellyn and Steph, apparently, had run 5:21.

"You're fat," Ben said, then burst out laughing.

"What did you just say?" Rochelle asked.

"I'm sorry," Ben said, palming his face. "I was going to say, 'You're fit,' but then I decided it might be a little premature, so I tried to change it to 'You're back,' and—well, you heard what came out."

"Ha! Justice!" I called out the window at Rochelle.

Back at the parking area everyone was in high spirits, the cool weather having given the whole team their best legs, it seemed.

"I heard you told Coach Ben you've never had more fun on two feet," Steph teased me. (This was true.) "You really need to get out more."

"'Don't allow anyone,'" I said, quoting Steph back to herself, "'to trivialize what running means to you.'"

In the afternoon I found myself sitting in front of my laptop at Matt's place with my eyelids at half-mast, the words on the screen dissolving into an unreadable blur. All the real pros on NAZ Elite take daily naps. I can't afford to take naps precisely because I'm not a real pro and I pay my bills by writing things like the thing I was currently trying to write for *Women's Running*. A few of my teammates have given me a hard time about not napping, contending that I can't claim to have had the full professional running experience until I've submitted to afternoon sleep. *Maybe now is the time*, I thought. But no, I had to meet my deadline.

I went downstairs and fixed myself a cup of coffee and drank it at my desk. Within minutes I was again seeing unreadable smudges on the screen in front of me. It was no longer a matter of choice. I flopped facedown on top of the bed that no slower runner than me has ever slept in and was out in seconds. When I woke up forty-five minutes later I felt like a new man.

13 Days to Chicago

On a normal day I don't start thinking about beer until around four o'clock in the afternoon. Today I thought about it the moment I woke up. That's because today is Day One of a two-week alcohol fast, self-imposed but inspired by Matt, the lifelong teetotaler, who, legend has it, convinced the entire University of Richmond men's cross country team to lay off the bottle for the duration of the 2010 season as a symbol of their shared commitment to qualifying for the NCAA championship, a goal they achieved, stone-cold sober, for the first time in a coon's age. I believe the legend, having heard it from Matt's own lips several weeks ago, in the kitchen, as I held a can of beer (I'd cut back to a few a week, but I hadn't gone full Matt Llano). I remember thinking then, *Heck, why not? I could do that*—for a couple of weeks, anyway, if only to shed a last pound or two. But, as psychology tells us, the surest way to think about a pink elephant is to tell yourself not to think about a pink elephant.

To distract myself from images of frosted pint glasses filled with frothy amber liquid, I logged on to Final Surge after breakfast to see if Coach Ben had posted my final two weeks of training before Chicago. He had! Skimming over the highlights (a set of mile repeats at Camp Verde on Thursday, two times three miles at marathon pace next Wednesday, also at Camp Verde), I moved the cursor over to October 8, hoping Ben had gone so far as to give me a pacing plan for the marathon itself, but the description box that opened up contained just one word of instruction: "Crush." No matter—we had an afternoon meeting scheduled to discuss that very topic.

An excruciating massage from Monica in the late morning brought further distraction, after which I dropped in at Kickstand Kafé, where Coach Ben was busily preparing for a visit from a trio of top executives from Hoka's French headquarters to deliver the team's new sponsorship contract. I found him at his favorite corner table, took a seat opposite him, and came right to the point.

"What did yesterday's workout tell you?" I asked, leaning in.

"The number is six-oh-five," Ben said.

Boom! There it was. Eleven weeks of dancing around the subject and now, in the time it takes a hip abductor tendon to snap, I had my wish. Catching my smile, Ben made a staying gesture with his right palm.

"Now, it so happens that six-oh-five is two thirty-nine marathon pace," he said. "But that's not how I chose it. Too many marathoners pick some arbitrary time they want to hit and then figure out what pace they have to run to meet their goal when what they should do is the opposite. I went with six-oh-five because it's the fastest pace I'm *one hundred percent certain* you can run for twenty-six point two miles. Do I think you might be able to run a little faster? Sure. But the smart way to get there is not to start the race at six flat if you're anything less than one-hundred percent confident you can keep it up all the way. What I want to see you do in Chicago is run six-oh-fives until *you* are one-hundred percent confident you can close faster. What do you think?"

"I like it," I said, still smiling.

In the evening, Nataki and I hung out in the TV room with Heather and James, who filled us in on their apartment hunt. At one point James leapt up from the sectional, disappeared briefly into the downstairs guest bedroom, and returned with an acoustic guitar.

"Rented this today," he said, grinning.

"Can you actually play it?" I asked.

"I'm going to play it tonight. They have an open mic every Monday at Hops on Birch. You guys should come."

I dropped my head like a football fan who's just watched his team's potentially game-winning field goal sail wide left.

"James, you know I love you," I said, "but the last place I want to go on my first night on the wagon is a bar. I'm sure you'll be great. The problem is, everyone else will probably suck, and I can't think of anything that would make me need a beer more than being forced to endure a bunch of awful singing."

At that moment Matt walked in the door, home from another trip to Phoenix to see John Ball.

"How's Day One going?" he called out to me, smiling tauntingly.

Last night, when Nataki and I returned to the house from Majerle's Sports Grill, where I savored my last cold one with Heather, James, and Big Dog, Matt expressed mock disappointment at my early return and chided me for failing to take proper advantage of my final hours of intemperance, reminding me that there were still a couple of Josh Bolton's leftover beers in the fridge.

"You're enjoying this, aren't you?" I said to him now.

11 Days to Chicago

The weather outlook for the Chicago Marathon is less than ideal. In a word: hot. I was fretting over the latest forecast this morning while bent over a bowl of granola and berries at the breakfast bar when Matt padded in, rubbing sleep from his eyes.

"Ready for the question of the day?" I asked.

"Go for it," he said resignedly.

Of the five marathons Matt has run, two took place in hot conditions: the Los Angeles Marathon in 2015 (high 70s) and the Olympic Trials Marathon in the same city the following year (low 70s). So I asked him now how he had prepared for these events.

"Physically or mentally?" he asked.

"Mentally, I guess."

"We just didn't make a big deal about it," Matt said as he began to whip up a batch of teff pancakes. "Our attitude was that the less we worried, the more of an advantage we had on runners who did."

Coach Ben has been watching the weather, too, and has instructed Brauny and me to prepare physically for the expected heat in Chicago by overdressing for our remaining runs in Flagstaff, which is why I left Matt's place two hours later wrapped in full tights, two top layers, and running gloves—overkill for a morning that was more cool than cold. My destination on this occasion was not Walnut Canyon or Woody Mountain Road or any of the other usual running venues but Craig's house in University Heights, an all but inevitable outcome of Ben's having allowed Craig to select today's route. On arriving, I found him at the kitchen table with a laptop before him, editing Ben Bruce's latest blog post, a recap of his summer of pain, hope, and heartbreak.

"He basically writes without punctuation," Craig said without judgment.

While my host searched for a good place to drop a comma, I wandered into the living room, which was cluttered with stacks of papers and piles of clean laundry and had the overall appearance of a home that had either just been moved into or was about to be moved out of, although, as far as I knew, Craig and his fiancée, Meg Bellino, have been there a while and are in no hurry to relocate. I closed my eyes and tried to picture the San Francisco apartment I lived in when I was twenty-four, and what came to me was an image of a battered wooden coffee table littered with CD cases, empty beer bottles, and pot-smoking paraphernalia.

Aaron showed up and went straight into his old man exercises, as Coach Ben calls them—a collection of dynamic stretches John Ball gave him to keep his wonky hip working. He was just finishing up when Craig joined us, having handed over his editing job to Meg with strict instructions not to be too heavy-handed with her corrections. Enjoying the rare opportunity to call the shots, the second-year pro led us outside and guided us through an improvised eight-mile loop that took us up to Fort Tuthill Park via Soldier's Trail, past the airport, then down to Lake Mary Road, onto Ranch Road toward Kellyn's place, and back to our starting point. We talked mostly about the looming visit from the Hoka bigwigs, during which (word was) they would have the opportunity to test some top-secret carbon-plated prototype racing flats, but near the end of the run I changed the subject with one of my patented grenade-like non sequiturs.

"Well, it appears Coach Ben likes me best," I proclaimed.

"How's that?" Craig said, taking the bait.

"It's obvious. Tomorrow I'm going down to Camp Verde to run and you guys are staying up here. Where's Ben going to be? That's right: with me!"

"Hate to burst your bubble," Craig said, "but Ben told me he's going down there to keep an eye on you so you don't blow the workout."

"Is that true?"

"Look! A bald eagle!" Craig said, pointing in a random direction.

I said no more, but in the privacy of my thoughts I vowed to prove to Coach Ben and my teammates that, despite all evidence to the contrary, I *can* pace myself like a real pro if I set my mind to it. To put him on notice, I texted Ben in the evening and offered to buy him lunch at Kickstand Kafé if I run a single interval more than two seconds off my target pace in either direction, slow or fast.

"I'll have the chorizo burrito," he replied.

10 Days to Chicago

Coach Ben and I talked about pacing for most of the forty-five minutes it took us to drive to Camp Verde this morning, our conversation picking up where yesterday's text message exchange left off.

"I know I've earned a rep for being terrible at hitting my times," I said as Ben piloted the Pilot down I 17, doing a steady eighty in a seventy-five zone, "but I was actually really good at pacing myself before I came here. Heck, my last four races have been negative splits."

Not to be outdone, Ben told me that when he was running for the Hansons, his feel for pace became so refined that he could guess his time for each lap around the track to within a few tenths of a second before looking at his watch.

"It's a real skill," I said. "If you think about it, what you just described is no less impressive than a quarterback dropping a forty-yard bomb into a streaking receiver's breadbasket. It just looks a little less spectacular on television."

"My theory is that it's mainly a matter of experience," Ben said in his teacher voice. "Most professional runners have been doing all the basic workout types for so long that hitting splits is second nature to them. Runners who start as adults don't have all that practice to fall back on."

I was tempted to point out that, as a forty-six-year-old runner who picked up the sport at age eleven, I have more experience than most real pros.

We parked at the same spot as last week. Ben pulled his trusty measuring wheel out of the back and walked a mile, placing cones at 200-meter intervals, while I warmed up. Just yesterday Ben was in Camp Verde with Faubs, Futsum, Kellyn, Matt, Rochelle, Scott Smith, and Steph, for whom he'd measured out the same mile. Too Slow has a theory that Ben does these things not because he's OCD but to set an example for the team—one of resisting complacency, not cutting corners, and attending to details.

I was nearing the end of my warm-up when I heard footsteps approaching from my rear. I knew by the sound alone—a soft, nippy tapping—that they were the footsteps of an elite runner even before a whippet of a young man with a stride so beautiful it seemed like an insult to my own whizzed by me.

"Did you see Diego Estrada?" Ben asked when I got back to the car.

Diego has run 1:00:51 for the half marathon and is on the elite start list of the Chicago Marathon. In other words, he's my competition.

I banged out my drills and strides and then walked to the first cone. Coach Ben positioned himself 100 yards ahead, next to a little drink station he'd set up for my use. The distance between us created some confusion about who was supposed to initiate the first interval, the result of which was that, just two strides into it, I heard Ben yell something—either "Go!" or "Stop!"—so I stopped. Ben threw up his arms.

"Did I just false start a fucking *workout*?" I laughed.

Our second attempt went off without a hitch. My job now was to run six times one mile in 5:55 on a minute's rest. If I completed a single mile in 5:58 or slower or in 5:52 or faster I owed Ben lunch. At 200 meters, with Ben now riding his mountain bike alongside me, I was dead on pace at 44 seconds. The number so pleased me that I sped up unwittingly and finished the mile in 5:53.5, according to Ben's watch.

"Dang it!" I growled. "Still, it's within the window."

Ben merely shrugged. Only then did I recall his rumored predilection for wagers and realize he might feel a bit conflicted—the coach in him wanting me to nail my times, the gamer wanting me to blow it.

A minute passed in what seemed like twelve seconds and I began to run back the way I'd come, trying to go just a teensy bit slower than I had the first time. At the half-mile cone (3:01) I discovered I'd overcompensated, so I sped up, overcompensated in the other direction, and completed the mile in 5:52.

"I guess I owe you lunch," I moped.

Ben did not gloat, not even a little, and I knew then that this was one wager he'd had no desire to win. Determined to do better—for my selfless coach if not for my hapless self—I set off again, vowing not to repeat the same mistake, and I didn't. I made the opposite mistake, hitting the midpoint in 2:56 (too fast) and finishing in 5:56 (too slow).

"Interesting," Ben observed.

I knew what "interesting" meant. It meant, *Dude, it's not that hard! Just run the damn time!* Ben kept this thought to himself, however, instead making a teachable moment of my failure with a warning against trying to make up for pacing errors on race day, when it counts.

"If you run the first mile too slow, don't run the second mile too fast to make up for it," he said. "Just focus on running each mile on pace no matter what you did in the last one."

I ran the fourth rep in 5:54.

"Better," Ben pronounced, his tone that of a patient piano teacher praising a hopeless pupil's least awful rendition of "Chopsticks."

"Well, my average is improving," I said, "but I still haven't run a single five fifty-five."

Having nothing left to lose, I stopped overthinking and just ran. My next mile was completed in 5:55.3, my last in 5:55.0.

"That's why we practice," Ben said.

9 Days to Chicago

John Ball worked his special voodoo on my legs one last time this afternoon. When he was through hurting me, we shook hands and he wished me luck in Chicago.

"Take it easy on me in your book," he said in lieu of goodbye.

After a quick stop at the hotel to freshen up, I ushered Nataki back out to the Fun Mobile and steered it to Ahwatukee, an area of south Phoenix, to search for an apartment we occupied together for eleven months at the turn of the millennium and hadn't seen since. The address was long gone from our memories, but I was confident I could locate the right property by cruising the streets whose names I did remember and scanning for familiar landmarks. Not so. On and on I drove, left, right, straight, becoming increasingly agitated until Nataki, rightly diagnosing low blood sugar as the proximal cause of the storm brewing in me, suggested we stop for dinner. Minutes later we were seated inside a small strip mall Thai restaurant, where my sanity was restored by means of yellow curry.

"I'm one hundred percent convinced I've been here before," I said to Nataki between sips of something that wasn't beer.

"There's a sign outside that says 'Grand Opening.'"

"I don't mean this restaurant. I mean this space—whatever was here back then. I think we should try again."

Nataki's noncommittal shrug was good enough for me, so we tried again, and again we drove on and on, left, right, straight, recognizing everything vaguely and nothing specifically. I felt like a polar explorer trying to locate his tent in a blizzard, agonized by the knowledge that his corpse would one day be found inches from safety. Feeling another meltdown coming on, I whipped the car around and sped back toward the hotel—and that's when I saw it: a stucco-faced constellation of buildings on our left side that, although it did not match the image I carried in my conscious memory, which rendered the property as newer, grander, and

162

more lusciously landscaped, did evidently match a deeper imprint stored in some pre-mammalian nook of my brain stem. Without thinking, I swung a hard turn across traffic, earning an angry honk from a misanthropic homebound commuter privately glad for the excuse to show his middle finger, and onto the grounds of a place now called Lore at South Mountain.

All at once, I remembered *everything*, an inner compass guiding me straight to guest parking, unmoved since 1999. Marching like twin somnambulists, Nataki and I got out of the car and cut a diagonal to our former unit, along the way discussing and dismissing the idea of knocking on the door and explaining ourselves to the current occupant, choosing instead to station ourselves at the best outside vantage for photo-taking.

No words can describe the aching blend of fond nostalgia and bittersweet sorrow I felt as we stood there like home-casing housebreakers contemplating a drab stucco wall, a nondescript entry door, and an unremarkable balcony rail that would have meant nothing to anyone else but that I saw as pieces of my life, like the long-dead cells that made up my body back then, heart-piercing symbols of the irrecoverableness of lost time. Eighteen years ago, I realized, almost to the day, when I was twenty-eight years old and Nataki and I inhabited this crummy-looking apartment that once seemed so high-class, I ran my first half marathon, a tune-up race for my debut marathon. The half went reasonably well, but the marathon itself was a disaster, as were most of the marathons that followed, calamities so varied in cause that as time passed I began to wonder if God just didn't want me to run a decent marathon.

There was Long Beach in 2002, where I started with a 6:18 mile and finished at a walk (overambitious pacing); Sacramento in 2007, where I started fresh off a 10K that predicted a marathon time of 2:37 but in fact completed in 2:47 (overtraining); Boston in 2007, where I started fresh off a half-marathon that predicted a marathon time of 2:34 but instead completed in 3:18 (inadequate preparation for the hills); and Los Angeles in 2011, where I started with high hopes of breaking 2:40 at long last at age forty but dropped out at mile eight (hip injury)—just to name a few.

Looking back, I couldn't help but wonder what the twenty-eight-year-old marathon virgin whose home I was now spying on would have thought if he'd been allowed to glimpse the athletic future that awaited him. More than likely, I imagined, he would have regarded it as an unthinkably cruel nightmare, a waste of potential so maddeningly unfair he might have quit running then and there to spare himself the experience. And yet, it struck me next, this is not at all how I actually feel now, having lived through all of these heartbreaks, because I am no longer that naïve young man.

They say youth is wasted on the young. I don't know if a 2:39 marathon would have been wasted on me at age thirty, but I do know that I will savor the achievement far more richly nine days from now, if it happens, than I would have then, for all it took, and how long. In fact, as an older man who's been given the unexpected gift of a brief second youth, I'm savoring the mere opportunity—the lacing of the shoes, the sweat on my brow, the mingling of other runners' shadows with mine on the sliding asphalt, every vanishing moment of the journey—in a way I never did when I was younger. For the young, there is always tomorrow. To live a dream is a wonderful thing at any age, but it is never treasured more than when there is no tomorrow.

"Are you ready to go?" Nataki asked.

"Not quite," I said.

OCTOBER

7 Days to Chicago

This morning James scored a rare victory in our daily race to the coffee maker. I didn't mind, in this instance, because the competition wasn't even close, and by the time I came downstairs James and Heather were seated at the breakfast bar, steaming mugs and bowls before them, eyes glued to James's laptop, and the Keurig was free.

"How are they doing?" I asked.

NAZ Elite had two representatives—Futsum and Martin Hehir (NAZ Elite's lone remote member)—in today's USA 10 Mile Championships, which were being hosted in Minneapolis and streamed live on usatf.tv.

"Just started," James said.

Emerging from his bedroom, Matt silently assessed the situation and transferred the live stream from James's small computer screen to his own giant TV monitor. I prepared my breakfast and joined the others on the sectional. Martin ended up eighth and Futsum tenth. The top six finishers were naturalized American citizens born in Kenya.

At eight o'clock I left the house, once again intentionally overdressed, and drove to Woody Mountain Road to meet up with Brauny and Craig for my final long run before the Chicago Marathon. Arriving first, I killed time by opening the internet browser on my phone and visiting the Twin Cities Marathon website to see how Michael Crouch was doing. Having run 2:21 previously, Michael was chasing the U.S. Olympic Trials qualifying standard of 2:19 on the same streets Futsum and Martin had just chased the Kenyan expats down.

His result, posted just as my teammates were rolling in, caused me to wince in empathetic pain, as when a football player's knee bends in the wrong direction. Running the second half of the race six minutes slower than the first, he finished in 2:28:21, a dream time for most runners, but Michael isn't most runners. I'd hit the wall in enough marathons to know how he must be feeling right about now—not only stunned and disappointed but also humbled, dreading his return to Flagstaff, where he'll hear the same commiserative clichés from everyone he knows.

Having survived eight miles with Aaron and Craig a few days ago, I had hopes of hanging on with them for fourteen miles today, but I was kidding myself. Their pace felt wrong from the start, and after a quarter mile I made the prudent but bitter-tasting decision to back off and run alone. A fierce headwind pestered me nonstop on the way out, inflating my early mile splits and stoking my bitterness. By Mile 4 I had reversed my prior opinion of Woody Mountain Road, losing all appreciation for its bosky serenity and charming fauna, seeing nothing now but its rutted, sandy surface, where you're always looking for a good place to plant your foot and never finding it.

A silver Jeep Patriot appeared in the distance, creeping toward me at about the speed of a marathon press truck before stopping some twenty feet away. Through the windshield I spied Big Dog at the wheel, his fiancé, Angela Gavelli (a massage therapist who worked on me once when Monica was unavailable), at his side. Normally I hate to interrupt a long run for anyone at any time, but this time I was more than happy to pause at Angie's open window.

"What are you doing out here?" I asked.

"Abdi's crushing a long run," Eric said, shooting a thumb in the direction they'd come from.

Abdi Abdirahman is a Flagstaff institution. Self-nicknamed the Black Cactus, he has represented the U.S. in four Olympics and has free-beer-for-life privileges at Mother Road Brewery, a dispensation he is reputed to make full use of. Now forty years old, he's currently training for the New York City Marathon.

"That makes one of us," I grumbled.

Big Dog drove off and I ran on. Soon a dusky stick figure came around a bend up the road, chugging along like James Brown's rhythm section. The Black Cactus in the flesh. We exchanged comradely head nods as we passed each other, and in that moment some kind of mystical energy transfer occurred (or so it seemed). In an instant I felt less victimized by my environment, more aware of the crisp fall weather and the sweeping vistas off to my right—of the gift of just being here, now, doing this.

After turning around at seven miles I felt the wind at my back, in more ways than one. With each passing mile I grew stronger and more relaxed, and as my strength rose my split times fell: 7:14, 7:04, 6:45. And then, all of a sudden, I knew that I was going to break 2:40 in Chicago. Didn't think it—*knew* it.

It's hard to explain. Something's just different this time. On the several past occasions when I toed a marathon start line hoping to break 2:40, I was doing just that: *hoping* to break 2:40. My confidence, though real, was grasping to some degree; there was a drop or two (or three) of *trying* to believe mixed in with the actual believing. But the confidence I have now feels received rather than reached for. I'm not as young as I used to be nor even as fast as I used to be, nor can I say that I am any fitter now than I have been a few times previously. Yet I've never felt this damn *good*, this sure, a week before a marathon.

On the homestretch, I spied Craig in the distance, leaning against the hood of his car, apparently waiting for me. I'd been wondering what the hell had happened to my teammates, whom I should have met head-on at some point. The moment I stopped, Craig began to apologize for disappearing on me, explaining that he and Aaron had gotten fed up with the dust that was being kicked up by passing vehicles (another annoyance) and broken away from the road, turning what had begun as an out-and-back into a loop, and that's why I hadn't seen them.

"So, how'd it go for you?" he asked.

A superstitious instinct tried to muzzle me, reminding me that the real pros let their running do the talking—and for good reason. What happened to Michael Crouch today can happen to anyone. Why risk making a potential bad day on the race course even worse by talking big beforehand? "Dude," I said, "I'm so ready!"

6 Days to Chicago

After failing to cross paths with man-about-town Abdi Abdirahman even once during my first twelve weeks in Flagstaff, I've now seen him two days in a row. This time we met properly, his friend Diane Nukuri—a Burundian pro I'd encountered a couple of times previously when she dropped in on team runs—introducing us shortly after the two of them arrived together in Abdi's black BMW M3 with tinted windows to join the NAZ Elite crew for an easy run at Walnut Canyon. Also present were Craig, Kellyn, James, Rochelle, and Steph, all of us (for once) intending to run the same distance.

I spent the better part of those eight miles in conversation with Kellyn, who'd had a bad weekend, failing a fitness test she took as part of her application for a firefighting job in Flagstaff. Passing it would have required that she complete a series of tasks that included shouldering a fire hose up several flights of stairs and dragging a 165-pound dummy (Kellyn herself weighs 110 pounds) thirty feet in less than three minutes. She missed the cutoff by twelve seconds.

"It's embarrassing," she seethed. "I hate knowing that by failing I confirmed some people's expectations for female firefighters."

"I get it," I said. "It's one thing to fail, another thing to fail in front of an audience. Heck, I worry about that for myself in Chicago. If I fall on my face, a lot of folks are going to know."

When we finished, Kellyn, true to form, cleared out immediately, leaving the rest of us to waste a little time chitchatting before we got on with our respective days.

"I'm retired," I heard Abdi say from his seat on the hood of his Beamer.

"What!" I said. "Are you serious?"

"He said 'tired,' not '*re*tired,'" Diane clarified.

"I hate being tired when I run," Abdi added tiredly.

"I hate being tired in general," Rochelle said.

"Actually, I kind of like being tired at bedtime," I chimed in.

"Me, too!" Rochelle amended, erupting in a childlike grin. "I like being tired at bedtime. Or when I have nothing to do."

"Like a cat," I said.

"Cats have the best life," Diane said dreamily.

We all fell silent, thinking about how great it would be to be a cat.

In the afternoon, back at Matt's place, a fog came over me, the same one that, eight days ago, overpowered my efforts at resistance (and caffeine) and all but forced me to experience the pro runner ritual of the afternoon nap. This time, though, I didn't even try to fight it.

5 Days to Chicago

All ten Flagstaff-based members of NAZ Elite (and one middle-aged tagalong) met at Brauny's house this morning for an easy run. Conscious of the approaching end of my fake pro runner experience, I took advantage of the opportunity by asking Jen Rosario to snap a group photo. Ben Bruce thought it would be funny if everyone flanked me at an awkward distance instead of crowding around with a couple of arms thrown chummily over my shoulders in the customary manner, but I insisted on playing it straight. Later, though, I kicked myself, realizing too late that there was no reason Jen couldn't have captured both poses, serious and goofy.

"That was a book cover, by the way," I said as we broke formation, eliciting a chorus of groans. "Hope your hair looked good."

We set off toward the Urban Trail, the initial sorting of bodies leaving me next to Futsum this time. Having not seen him since his race on Sunday, I asked how his legs were feeling.

"Pretty good," he said. "Not too beat-up. How about you? It's race week, man! I'm excited for you and Aaron."

"I'm bouncing off the walls," I said. "I've never been more geeked up for a race."

"You're running for your mother, right?"

Shortly after her diagnosis, I posted a tweet dedicating my race to her. I hadn't known Futsum paid attention to that sort of thing.

"I am indeed," I affirmed.

"That's good. But there are twenty-six miles in a marathon. I think you should also run one mile for each of us."

Futsum made a lassoing motion with his finger to indicate whom he meant by "us," which was everyone.

"I will," I said, my voice thickening. "I want to make you guys proud."

Ben Bruce—running for the first time in five days—was the only runner besides me who'd been assigned just four miles this morning, so the two of us peeled away from the group at two miles and began to make our way back toward our starting point. Along the way, we came to a neighborhood park that had a couple of portable toilets. Ben made a sour face and told me to go on without him, as he might be a while.

"When it rains, it pours," he said cryptically.

Back at Aaron's house, neither Nataki nor the Fun Mobile was anywhere to be seen. Puzzled, I stood around uselessly until Ben approached.

"Nataki's at the park," he said before I could ask.

"Oh, good," I said. "I was a little worried."

Ben looked like he had more to say. I waited.

"She was in the port-o-potty," he confessed. "The door was unlocked. I walked in on her. Saw her butt."

I didn't know whether to laugh or cry.

"We must never again speak of this," I said.

Nor did Nataki and I speak of it during the drive back to Matt's place. But the moment we walked through the front door, Matt called out to us, and I feared that news of the embarrassing incident had leaked. I needn't have worried.

"Check this out!" he said as we entered the kitchen. "This" was a plastic water bottle that looked to me like a space-age dildo—its shape a hybrid of torpedo and hourglass, the shaft bright blue, the head vibrant green.

"What is it?" I asked.

"It's the bottle I was telling you about that I found online. UPS just brought it. I might use it in Frankfurt."

"It looks, um, phallic," I said.

James and Heather giggled from their seats at the breakfast bar. Matt turned crimson.

"Oh no!" I teased. "I've ruined it. You'll never be able to bring yourself to drink out of that thing now."

"Actually, it makes me *more* inclined to use it," Matt countered.

The room exploded in laughter.

"It appears Matt Llano is drinking from a giant penis," Matt said in the voice of a television commentator.

I doubled over, laughing till my ribs hurt, stopping only when I remembered that tomorrow is my last full day in Flagstaff. My last day like this day.

4 Days to Chicago

Nataki and I came downstairs this morning to find Rochelle sitting at the kitchen table spooning oatmeal from a bowl she'd fixed at home and brought with her to Matt's place. Matt himself sat at the breakfast bar with his full attention on his phone.

"Good morning," Nataki said to him.

Receiving no response, Nataki shook him playfully by the shoulders and repeated her greeting.

"I *said* 'Good morning!'" he protested. "Why do people always think I ignore them? Aaron gets mad at me about it all the time, and I'm like, 'You need to check your ears. I always say hi back when you say hi."

Nataki and I exchanged a look. More than once we have discussed our host's habit of ignoring our greetings, something Nataki takes personally and I dismiss as unintentional.

"Where is everyone?" I asked.

"Probably outside," Matt said, still sounding aggrieved. "For some reason no one ever wants to come in."

"Probably because you ignore them," I said.

Matt squinched his eyes at me and said nothing more.

I went to the front door and poked my head out. Sure enough, the whole crew was assembled on the sidewalk: Craig, Kellyn, Steph, Too Slow, and Coach Ben. Minutes later, we were back on the road to Camp Verde, Ben's Pilot leading the way with the Fun Mobile following, though by now I knew the way blindfolded. Docking at the usual location, we emerged from the vehicles with the energy of birdwatchers and quietly set about our individual ready-making routines. The morning air was comfortably cool, but I went ahead and stripped down to shorts and a singlet, having checked the forecast, which called for an afternoon high of 92.

"I thought you were in heat training," Craig said as I stuffed my sweat-clothes inside the back hatch.

"I am," I said. "It's going to be ninety-two today."

When the last of the stretching mats had been stashed away, we trotted off, hogging the otherwise empty road like a pack of stray cattle. Sensing eyes on me, I glanced left and saw Steph looking me up and down.

"I thought you were in heat training," she said, having evidently missed my earlier exchange with Craig.

"Anyone else have something to say about my clothes?" I grumbled.

Coach Ben's go-to final pre-marathon tune-up consists of two times three miles at goal pace. Pretty basic. Brauny, who likes to stay close to home before races, elected to do the workout on his own in Flagstaff, and everyone else had speed work today, so it was just Coach Ben and I who made the short jaunt to the start of the three-mile loop I'd become familiar with on my first trip to Camp Verde.

"Okay, no more screwing around," Ben said. "I want to see 6:05s straight through. This isn't for my benefit—it's for yours."

I signaled my understanding with a mute nod and Ben sent me off. Recalling what 5:55 pace felt like last week, I tried to feel my way to a speed that was precisely 1.3 percent lower, something my real-pro teammates seem able to do with ease. Ben pulled up alongside me as I hit the first cone in ninety-one seconds.

"So far, so good!" he called out.

He was beside me again when I passed the second cone at 3:02.

"It's a miracle!" Ben shouted.

Finding me still locked in at 1,200 meters, Ben zoomed away to check on the others. I saw him again, though, at the two-mile cone (which sat conveniently at the foot of the spur the others were running 400s on), where I cruised by at 12:10 flat, and once more at the finish, where I stopped the clock at 18:15.

"Dude!" Ben said, shaking his head in wonder.

Having gained my coach's confidence, I was allowed to run the second loop unsupervised and managed not to get too carried away, cranking out back-to-back-to-back 6:03s. I cooled down with Craig, who'd run a bunch of solo 800s to sharpen up for the half marathon he's racing on Sunday in San Jose, and then waited with him for the other members of my carpool to finish up their workout. Not until we were all about to leave did I realize I might be seeing some of my teammates for the last time.

"Well, I guess this is goodbye," I said.

"You're ready," Kellyn said, offering me an awkward one-armed hug that was actually more than I'd expected from her.

"Thanks," I said.

"Don't start too fast," Steph said, giving me the same half embrace.

Rochelle followed suit with a sideways hug of her own, and then our paths diverged, for who knows how long.

Shit was getting real, and it got even realer three hours later, when I sat down with Coach Ben at his dining room table for a pre-race planning session, something he does with each of his runners before important races.

MATT FITZGERALD

"One thing I think you need to be prepared for is the hype and energy of being in that elite corral," he began. "It's going to be a little different than anything you've experienced, and there's probably going to be a lot of adrenaline pumping through you."

"I can only imagine," I said.

"Try to soak in that energy and bottle it up for later. When the race begins, do what you're prepared to do. Try to hit a six-oh-five. If you don't, try to hit a six-oh-five. If you don't, try to hit a six-oh-five."

I laughed. Ben didn't.

"Seriously, though. Don't start compensating and trying to do the math in your head. Just keep trying to hit a six-oh-five every single mile."

"Well, perhaps not *every* mile," I countered.

"True. It's a matter of being patient, waiting until at least thirty K and then making a decision: 'Okay, do I think I can squeeze it down a bit? And if I do squeeze it down, can I go all the way to the finish?' If the answer is 'No,' or 'I'm not sure,' then you just keep waiting until you *are* sure. The only thing I'm even remotely worried about with you is that you'll misjudge that piece."

"I won't let you down, Coach," I said.

"It's not just about being patient and smart, though," Ben continued. "At a certain point, it becomes a matter of guts. Let's be honest: To do the best you possibly can in a marathon, you're going to have to hurt at some point."

"Trust me," I said. "If I get to that point and I know I still have a chance to break two forty, I won't care how much it hurts."

In the evening, I hosted a send-off party for myself at The Cottage, where Matt, James, and Heather joined Nataki and me at a candlelit table in a cozy nook. When our drinks arrived, I raised my glass of seltzer and saluted James on making it to age thirty-six (his birthday was last Sunday) and then thanked Matt for putting up with my endless questions for three months. James tried to add a toast to my success in Chicago, but I shushed him.

"Today's not about me," I said magnanimously. Pause. "Every other day is about me!"

Nataki has had to endure a lot of running talk this summer, and she graciously absorbed one more round as we tucked into our appetizers.

"There's something I've been wanting to ask you," I said to Matt, who was seated across from me. "Consider it my final Question of the Day."

"I'm all ears," Matt said, his fork probing in an exploratory fashion at the sweetbreads he'd gamely ordered on a tag-team dare from James and me.

"Would you invest as much as you do in running if you were as slow as me?"

Matt chewed longer than seemed necessary, either giving the delicacy a chance or buying time.

"Well, obviously I wouldn't be running professionally if that were the case," he said carefully. "But I do still think I would put a lot of time and energy into it, because I love it. In fact, that's kind of what I did. As you know, I wasn't the greatest runner in high school or college. Most of my peers who were running at my level then didn't even try to turn pro."

"It bothers me that so many runners feel they somehow don't *deserve* to take the sport all the way and find out how good they can be," I said. "I wish more folks with average talent would just go for it."

Heather raised her right arm overhead like a star pupil who knows the answer. We all looked at her.

"You just described me to a 'T,'" she said. "For a long time I was stuck at three forty-five to three forty in the marathon, and the whole reason I was stuck there was that I didn't think I was good enough to work with a coach or do foam rolling every day or eat better. But, of course, the whole reason I wasn't good enough was that I wasn't doing these things! I was caught in a self-limiting mindset."

"What changed it?" I asked.

"It was this guy," Heather said, putting an arm around James's shoulder and drawing him in for a smooch.

"Who knows?" I said. "If I don't blow it on Sunday, maybe I can be that guy for a lot of runners. Minus the kissy part."

3 Days to Chicago

I was the very last passenger to board American Airlines Flight 3025, having badly misjudged how long it would take to get through security at tiny Flagstaff Pulliam Airport. Head bowed to avoid contact with the low ceiling of the Phoenix-bound puddle jumper, I made my way toward the rear of the cabin in search of seat 17A. When I got to Row 17 I discovered that the aisle seat (B) was occupied by a frizzy-haired young man whose attention was on his phone. Sensing my presence, he looked up, and I'll be damned if it wasn't Feyisa Lilesa, a professional runner from Ethiopia who generated international headlines last year by making a gesture of political protest as he crossed the finish line of the Olympic Marathon in second place, earning himself a silver medal and permanent exile from his homeland in a single moment. He now lives in Flagstaff on asylum.

Not one to waste such an opportunity, I introduced myself as soon as we were both buckled in.

"Are you going to Chicago?" Feyisa asked.

"Yes," I said.

"Are you running the marathon?"

"Yes."

"Do you live in Flagstaff?"

"No, I'm from California, but I've spent the summer in Flagstaff training with Northern Arizona Elite."

The name clearly meant nothing to Feyisa.

"White people all look the same to me," he offered cheerfully. "I go to the supermarket and somebody says, 'Hi, Feyisa,' and I think, 'Who are you?'"

I laughed, making a mental note to share the remark with Nataki (a reluctant flyer, who's staying behind for this one) when we Facetimed later.

"Who did you work with?" Feyisa asked.

By "work" he meant "train," I assumed, so I reiterated that I had trained with NAZ Elite and got the same blank look of nonrecognition.

"I worked with Abdi," Feyisa said. "When you come back to Flagstaff you should work with us and you will improve."

"I *did* improve!" I protested, feeling defensive of my team.

"What is your strategy?" Feyisa asked.

"Well, I'm an old man, not a real professional," I hedged. "My goal is to run two thirty-nine, *maybe* two thirty-seven if the weather improves." Feyisa has run 2:04:52. He showed no further interest in my running.

The plane took off and our conversation moved on to the topics of Ethiopian food, culture, and politics, steered in this direction by my mention of Futsum, whose Eritrean people share a kind of solidarity with Feyisa's people, the Oromo, based on their respective histories of persecution at the hands of Ethiopia's dominant powers.

"Ethiopians are very generous," Feyisa told me. "We will give you our last piece of bread if you are hungry. But if I go back there, the government will kill me."

More interested in Feyisa the runner than in Feyisa the activist, I asked him how many times he had run Chicago. He showed me three fingers.

"But this time, no pacers," he said. "When I ran two-oh-four in 2012, we had pacers. This time I must sleep." Feyisa made a pillow of his hands and rested a cheek against it. "Sleep for twenty K, thirty K, *then* race."

I got it: His strategy was to be patient. I told Feyisa that I, too, intended to sleep through the early part of the race.

The flight from Flagstaff to Phoenix takes just twenty-three minutes. We were already descending when I pulled up the race-day Chicago weather forecast on my phone (sunny, high of 78) and showed it to Feyisa.

"What do you think?" I asked.

"For me it's no problem," he said, curling his lip like an Italian mobster. "It's the same for everyone. You have to be prepared." He put a finger to his temple to indicate that he meant mentally prepared.

"You told me white people all look the same to you," I said to my new friend as we deplaned. "Will you know me if I see you on the start line Sunday?"

"I will know you," he said.

The odds of this happening got better when Feyisa and I boarded the same flight from Phoenix to Chicago, again sitting in the same row, and they got better still when we both joined a small group of VIPs awaiting limo rides in the baggage claim area at O'Hare, a group that also included Brauny, Sarah and Michael Crouch, Diego Estrada, and Diego's coach, the legendary Joe Vigil. An inveterate raconteur, eighty-seven-year-old Joe was ten minutes into a twenty-minute story about how he finagled his way to the 1968 Olympics in Mexico City when he was interrupted by the approach of a man dressed in a Chicago Marathon jacket. Seeming to know everyone else, our greeter quickly focused his attention on me.

"What's your name?" he asked.

I spoke my name and then watched with a sinking heart as the official studied a sheet of paper pinned to the clipboard he held.

"I'm afraid you're not on the list."

"That's unfortunate," I said.

"Wait a minute. What's your name again?"

I repeated it, silently praying that what I thought was coming was.

"I'm a huge fan!" the official said. "I've read many of your books. Don't worry, I'll get you to your hotel. But you must put me in your next book."

"What's *your* name?" I asked.

"Sebastian," he said, flashing a lanyard slung around his neck.

"Consider it done."

Feeling my companions' eyes on me, I turned around just in time to catch Sarah smirking at me.

"Here, miss, take this for me," I said, handing her my suitcase.

2 Days to Chicago

After a bagel breakfast (whole wheat, of course) at Einstein Bros., a four-mile run along Lakeshore Drive, a round of rehab exercises, a token stint of computer time, and a sandwich-and-salad lunch at Panera, I walked a mile and a half from the Hotel Chicago, where I'm lodging at my own expense, to the Hilton on Michigan Avenue, where most of the real pros are being put up for free, to check in for the race. According to the elite athlete welcome letter Josh Cox sent me a few days ago, the elite athlete registration area and hospitality suite were located on Floor T1, which turned out to be the twenty-fifth and top floor of the ninety-year-old high-rise. Josh had offered to meet me there to make sure everything went smoothly, but (true to form) I arrived early, so to kill time I wandered over to the hospitality suite, entering just as Steve Jones, winner of the 1985 Chicago Marathon and a former marathon world record holder, exited.

I passed through an anteroom dominated by a cloth-covered serving table laden with coffee, tea, water, Gatorade, snack bars, and cookies, and emerged into a larger space containing a massive formal dining table surrounded by eight wide chairs and three separate sitting areas, one of them arranged around a built-in media center with a television showing the film *Bruce Almighty* on mute. In the chair closest to the screen sat a lean, silver-haired man wearing the same Chicago Marathon polo shirt I'd seen on Sebastian at the airport.

"Hey, NAZ Elite!" he called out, noticing my own shirt. "Are you guys all in town?"

Acting on the assumption that my welcomer was an important individual who had a right to the information he'd just requested, I took a seat and informed him that Aaron Braun and I arrived yesterday, and Ben Rosario was on his way.

"And you are . . . ?"

In as few words as possible, I explained the whole fake pro runner thing, whereupon the silver-haired man introduced himself as Chris Mengel, a sports agent for Elite Runner Management. Just then, Deena Kastor, winner of the 2005 Chicago Marathon, sauntered into the room and casually joined us, at which point Chris lost all interest in me and I became a mere spectator as he and Deena caught up. I was beginning to wonder if Deena even remembered me from our few past encounters when she abruptly addressed me.

"What brings you to Chicago?"

I started again to explain the whole fake pro runner thing, but the moment Deena understood I'd be racing with an elite bib on Sunday she leapt from the sofa and gave me a stinging high five.

"That is so cool!"

Encouraged by Deena's enthusiasm, I shared a bit more about my experience with NAZ Elite, but she cut me off a second time.

"You know what you should do?"

"Tell me," I said warily.

"You should run with Feyisa Lilesa as long as you can. That would make a hell of a story, don't you think?"

"Perhaps," I said. "But it would be a very short story."

Alberto Salazar was the next household name in the running world to pass through, pausing for a brief, stilted conversation with Deena before moving on. I felt a little sorry for him. Always gracious in my journalistic interactions with him, Alberto has sullied his reputation in recent years by bending the rules of fair play in his role as coach of the Nike Oregon Project, whose star runner, Galen Rupp, is widely favored to win on Sunday, and in environments such as this one he must feel as though he's sprouted horns and a tail.[*]

Noting the time, I wandered over to the registration room, where I took a chair at a long table opposite Laurie, a race staffer who handed me a number of forms to fill out, including one that let the event organizer know where to send my check in the event that I won prize money. I was already halfway through the process when Josh breezed in and sat down beside me. I showed him my race number, which was 33.

"Check it out," I said. "Two digits!"

---

[*] Note that this encounter occurred before Alberto Salazar was banned from coaching for four years by the U.S. Anti-Doping Authority for doping violations and before accusations of psychological abuse were levied against him by some of his former athletes.

"That's a great number," Josh said. "Are you going to try to beat it?"

In marathons, "beating your number" means beating everyone with a higher bib number and at least one with a lower number. The thirty-second finisher in last year's Chicago Marathon ran 2:24:07.

"I've got one number in my head, and that's not it," I said.

Laurie handed me a couple of Chicago Marathon-branded keepsakes: a backpack and a hooded sweatshirt. "That one's a small," she said in reference to the hoodie, "but you can have any size you like."

Before I left Matt's house yesterday I weighed in at 141.2 pounds, nine pounds down from my starting weight and the lightest I've been since I was in high school, which was the last time I wore a small anything. I tried on the sweatshirt. It fit.

"Do you have any questions?" Laurie asked.

Assuming that any real pro would have at least one question, I asked Laurie if music devices were permitted in the elite warm-up area. She said they were.

Josh and I pushed back our chairs and rose to leave.

"Oh, one more thing," Laurie said. "We're asking all of the elite runners to sign that commemorative poster on the table outside. Would you mind?"

Would I mind! Ha! I scrawled my name with gusto just below that of two-time marathon world champion Abel Kirui as Josh looked on, nodding approvingly.

"Thank you again for making this happen," I said to him on our way toward the elevators.

He waved a hand at my words of gratitude. "The best way to thank me is by running the race of your life on Sunday."

Josh jabbed the elevator call button and we turned to face each other.

"The marathon is such an opportunity," he said. "It's not merely twelve weeks of preparation. Your whole life goes into it. I know it's a cliché, but it's true: You run the first twenty miles with your head and the last six with your heart. You have to be smart in the first twenty. The less emotion you feel, the better. But when it gets hard and it's time to grind, that's when you pour everything you have into it—all your hopes and dreams, your failures and successes, your passion and fears, and all the sacrifices, big and small, you've made over the weeks and months and years to get to where you are right now, in the best and worst moment of an opportunity you won't be able to live with yourself if you don't seize."

"Dang, man!" I said. "That was a hell of a pep talk!"

"Actually, it's all written down on a postcard I was planning to give you later," he confessed. "But I mean every word of it."

A bell dinged and a pair of doors slid apart. Josh shook my hand and stepped in. Having completed my major tasks for the day, I returned to the hospitality suite to feel special. I was relaxing in a wingback chair with a cup of hot black coffee, trying not to think about the dishes of peanut M&M's and Lara Bars (tomorrow—carb-loading day—will be another matter), when I received a text message, to which I replied immediately.

Coach Ben: Everything okay so far?

Me: Yes. But it's possible I'm only dreaming all of this.

1 Day to Chicago

This morning I completed my final training run as a fake professional runner, a three-mile shakeout with James and Heather and a couple dozen clients of James's online coaching business who are also racing tomorrow. Afterward, back in my room, I made a quick call to my parents, as any son might do on the eve of a momentous occasion in his life—the birth of a child, open-heart surgery, spaceflight—or, in this case, competing in a World Major Marathon as an undeserving yet official registrant in the elite division.

"Go get 'em, boy!" Dad said.

"Be safe, honey," Mom told me.

Around noon, after completing the surprisingly tedious exercise of mixing up and labeling eight bottles of Maurten in two concentrations, I left the hotel again to do some things that only professional (and fake professional) runners have to do the day before a marathon, beginning with getting my uniform checked and dropping off my bottles at the Hilton. The elite athlete guide I picked up from Laurie during check-in yesterday directed me to the Mobley Room, one of those low-ceilinged all-purpose spaces with calculatedly ugly institutional carpeting. Inside I came to a folding table marked "Uniform Inspection," behind which sat three laughing race staffers.

"You folks seem to be enjoying yourselves," I said.

"Hey, if you have to do an asshole job, you might as well have fun with it," said the bearded one, provoking more laughter from his colleagues.

I pulled my uniform out of my backpack and placed it on the table for inspection. A woman measured the logos on the singlet with a ruler.

"Congratulations, you passed!" she said.

All four walls of the Mobley Room were lined with additional folding tables staffed by volunteers. I was instructed by the merry uniform inspectors to make my way around counterclockwise, depositing one of my eight bottles at each table. The woman at the next table showed me a schematic diagram of the elite aid station layout. She ran an index finger along it until she found my name, then tapped twice.

"Your bottle will be at the very end of the first table at each station," she said. "You're welcome to take a photo with your phone."

I would never have thought to do so, but supposing a real pro would, I did.

I had just dumped off my eighth and last bottle when Brauny entered. Things did not go quite as smoothly for him. The Hoka logo on his hat was larger than allowed, so the bearded guy covered it with thick white tape. Asked to produce his warm-ups for inspection, Aaron confessed he hadn't brought them. He gave the inspectors a pleading look, but to no avail—he had to fetch the garments. I understood then what was meant by "asshole job."

At half past three a technical meeting for elite athletes was held in the media center, which occupied the Continental Ballroom, an even larger showcase for ugly carpeting located on the basement level of the hotel. Spotting an open seat next to Sarah Crouch near the back, I took it.

"Thanks for the text," I said. "I don't know why you're so nice to me."

Earlier, while I was passing some more time in the elite athlete hospitality suite, I'd received the following message from Sarah:

> You're ready, Matt. The work is 99% done and all that's left is for you to put your body on autopilot and just do what your training has prepared you for. See you on the other side tomorrow!

"I'm being nice to you now," Sarah said, "because I'm going to take you to the woodshed tomorrow."

The meeting began. Tracey Wilson, whom the elite athlete guide identified as the marathon's "manager of elite athlete and participant programs," took the stage and led the gathering through a slideshow-illustrated litany of dos and don'ts for tomorrow. A substantial portion of the material (such as Tracey's request that whoever wins the race *not* stop their watch at the finish line, which would spoil the photo) was irrelevant to me, but I picked up some useful nuggets, including the existence of a blue tangent line marking the shortest distance from the start to the finish of the racecourse.

When the meeting broke up, Sarah and I remained seated, trading jockish banter while the crowd began to file out. As Feyisa passed, our eyes met, and he smiled in recognition. I smiled back.

Just outside the room another clipboard-armed race official stood sentry-like, scanning the throng for elite athlete lanyards and detaining their wearers one by one. When my turn came, the official explained that she was checking names against a list of runners selected for random drug testing. I found myself hoping (uniquely, I'm sure) my name *would* be on the list—for the experience—but alas, it was not.

Coach Ben, Brauny, and I had agreed to meet up for the elite athlete pasta dinner at five o'clock in the room next to the one we'd just left. I spent the intervening half hour in a quiet lounge area with Cindy Kuzma, a Chicago-based running journalist and friend who wanted to interview me about my recent adventures for asweatlife.com.

"What's been the most surprising thing so far?" she asked.

"How much I've improved," I said readily. "I don't know if it was the altitude, or the coaching, or the team environment, or the diet tweaks, or the physical therapy, or whatever else. Probably all these things made a difference. In any case, no matter how things turn out tomorrow, what I've experienced in Flagstaff has already redefined my notion of what's possible—not just for me, but for any runner willing to take it all the way."

"Wow, that's pretty profound," Cindy said. "But how do you share this message so that it has the same kind of impact on runners who haven't experienced what you have?"

"Simple," I said. "I'm just going to tell the story."

Race Day

My primary alarm (cell phone) went off at 4:15 A.M., my secondary alarm (clock radio) a minute later. I didn't need either of them, having woken at 4:08 with a full bladder and gone straight from the bathroom to the coffee maker to begin a well-practiced pre-race routine of heating water for instant oatmeal, scarfing a banana and a bottle of Ensure, slipping into my race uniform and warm-ups, visiting the bathroom again, and triple-checking that my backpack contained everything else I needed (racing flats, extra socks, caffeine pills, beet juice shot, iPod and earbuds, fun size bag of M&M's for the start line, elite athlete schedule).

I left the room at 4:48, the click of the door latch behind me triggering an involuntary shudder, an endocrine-level recognition of the intense living I would do, for better or worse, before I passed through the same door again. Seven floors down, the hotel's revolving entry spun me out into predawn air that wasn't quite as cool as I would have liked. Moving at a semibrisk pace that compromised between my eagerness to get where I was going and the need to conserve energy, I traced a previously rehearsed route to Palmer House, where I had been instructed to catch a bus that would transport elite athletes who were not lodging at the Hilton to the host hotel for transfer to other buses bound for the start area. I felt a small release of tension, like when you see your suitcase finally emerge from the chute at baggage claim, on arriving at the hotel's Monroe Street entrance, mentally checking off another item in the morning's complex logistics, grateful to soon be joining the throng of nervous athletes inside.

But there was no throng of nervous athletes inside, only a marble-floored foyer as still and hushed as a museum at midnight. Tamping down a reflexive upsurge of alarm, I took a seat on an antique bench, willing others to appear, becoming more certain by the second that I was not where I was supposed to be.

Then I remembered the schedule. I fished it out of the backpack and learned what I should have known already—that elite athletes were requested to present themselves on the *Wabash Street* side of Palmer House. After a quick glance at my watch, I burst outside and rounded the corner of Monroe and Wabash at a non-energy-conserving run, eyes fixed on the glorious image of a school bus idling at the curb. Bounding aboard, I plopped down directly behind the driver, melting in relief.

We reached the Hilton at 5:30, right on schedule. I exited first, leading an orderly file of elites and VIPs through a gauntlet of grave-faced race officials who directed us to an area where the rest of the pros—those who'd slept at the Hilton—were congregated, a ritual that in its tight choreography and sober pomp conjured images of prizefighters making their way to the ring for a title match. The first familiar faces I saw belonged to Sarah and Michael Crouch.

"You know how we agreed we needed to work on our trash talk?" Sarah said.

I told her to go ahead and get it over with.

"I'm here to chew gum and kick your ass. And I'm all out of gum."

"That one's older than I am," I said. "And anyway, you *do* have gum. You're chewing it now."

"Good point," Sarah conceded.

Josh Cox and Coach Ben appeared and greeted me in the gently upbeat tone that people use with loved ones in hospital beds. We were soon interrupted by orders to move outside and take our pick of a pair of chartered coaches. When the last passenger was seated, the door hinged, a hydraulic sigh was heard, and we began to roll toward Grant Park, a phalanx of four police motorcycles leading the slow procession, lights flashing. Nose to the window, I stared into a darkness teeming with runners and race volunteers all walking in one direction along the sidewalk under the stark light of streetlamps, many staring back at us with a curiosity bordering on awe. I was almost (but not quite) embarrassed by the thrill I felt at being mixed up with the true objects of their veneration.

The trip took all of five minutes, or about a minute longer than it would have taken on foot. The doors swung open and again we were trooped out and ushered forth with military efficiency, this time to a large tent filled with folding chairs arranged in rows. Brauny took a seat up front and I sat two chairs over, close but not too close. Coach Ben joined us a couple of minutes later and gave us the lowdown.

"It's six o'clock now," he said. "They're going to call you to the line at ten past seven. I suggest you start your warm-up at six forty-five. Aaron, you'll want to get your old-man exercises done before then. They have a stretching area in the back. Fitz, do whatever you normally do."

My instinct was to fill the gap by chatting with my teammate, but for all I knew he preferred to be left alone in such moments. I decided to feel him out.

"Do you choose any kind of power word or mantra for your marathons?" I asked.

"Not really," Aaron said. "I do pick songs to play in my head. For this race I picked Kendrick Lamar's 'Humble' for the first twenty miles and The Killers' 'I'm the Man' for the last ten K."

"I do mantras," I said. "Today's is just one word: 'Execute.'"

Gripped by sudden bowel pressure, I fled the tent and ducked inside one of several portable toilets (nearly all of them unoccupied) that stood in a row within the protected confines of the VIP zone—the greatest perk yet of the pro runner experience. When I got back to my seat, Brauny was gone, having moved to the stretching area to loosen up. I passed a quiet few minutes debating whether to ask 5000-meter world record holder Tirunesh Dibaba for a selfie (ultimately deciding against it) and then lowered myself to the ground and "did what I normally do," beginning with the strap-assisted hip flexor stretch Matt showed me on my first day with the team. At 6:44, Aaron returned and solemnly stripped down to his uniform, and I did the same.

We exited the tent on the far side, emerging into a grassy area limned by a concrete path around which runners were striding in lawless confusion, with no apparent agreement on which direction to go or which side to stay on. Choosing the counterclockwise-moving stream, we slipped in and tried our best to find a smooth rhythm despite the surrounding chaos. Sensing a runner crowding us from behind, I swiveled my head around and recognized the tailgater as Jordan Hasay, America's top hope for a victory on the women's side. Aaron and I moved aside to let her pass.

We circled in silence, our lack of interaction turning my attention inward, where I made the happy discovery that my legs had been secretly replaced during the night with those of a younger, fitter, faster runner.

"My legs feel really go-od!" I sang out in a boyish falsetto.

Brauny laughed appreciatively, and I knew then for certain that he was not unhappy for my company.

After three or four more circuits, a race official announced it was time to head over to the start line. Back inside the tent, I changed into my Tracers, stuffed everything I didn't need into my number-marked backpack for the organizers to look after, and joined the promenade of elite runners walking toward the racecourse. To our left were the corrals, now packed like cattle pens with amateur runners who studied us with a mixture of reverence and envy as we passed. There were approximately 40,000 of them, exactly 48 of us, and I thought, *This is fucking surreal.*

Between the corrals and the start line, a short stretch of pavement had been cordoned off for our exclusive use. Following the others' lead, I found a bit of open real estate and did my drills—the same sequence Coach Ben had hazed me with back in July. I was just about to show off my much-improved B skips when a runner stretching his thigh to my immediate right lost his balance and tumbled into me. It was Feyisa. He began to apologize but, recognizing me again, he grinned instead and shook my hand.

"Good luck," I said.

"You, too," he said.

The push-rim racers were sent off at 7:15. When they were safely out of sight, our group was let loose to run strides. Among the last to take advantage of the opportunity, I narrowly avoided colliding head-on with Abel Kirui as I accelerated down Michigan Avenue and he came in hot from the other direction.

Ordered back behind the line, we stood twitching and shaking like victims of a mass Ritalin overdose while the national anthem was belted out by an operatic soprano. With her satiny final A note still echoing in our ears, we were called forward and the first corral was opened, allowing the top-seeded amateurs to rush in from our rear. I positioned myself with due deference in the back row of elites, some ten feet from the timing mat. Third from the left in row one was Brauny. Feeling my eyes on him, he turned in search of me and mirrored my two-finger salute. He seemed unafraid.

"Two minutes," said the emcee.

Suddenly remembering my M&M's, I removed the tiny packet from the tiny pocket in my tiny shorts and gobbled its contents, my wandering gaze eventually landing on a television camera on the far side of the line. It was looking right back at me, like a rifle scope sighting a discovered imposter.

The gun sounded and we surged forward. Six steps into the race, I realized with brutal suddenness that my pro runner fantasy was essentially over. Although I still had the elite aid stations to look forward to, the real elites, male and female, were already galloping away from me as I was engulfed by a tide of my fellow hobbyists. Among them was Alex Harrison, who positioned himself on my right shoulder. He said something that I didn't quite catch, and I made no reply, letting my erstwhile long-run companion know that I was all business today.

After a quarter mile we entered a tunnel, the warmth inside it a foretaste of what the open air would feel like in an hour or so. James had warned me that GPS data is unreliable in Chicago even outside the city's satellite-blocking underpasses, so I ignored the Current Pace reading on my watch and looked ahead to the first official distance marker for a chance to gauge my pace.

It soon appeared: a white sign marked 1K. Having worked out the math beforehand, I knew the number I wanted to see on my watch when I got there—3:46—the metric equivalent of 6:05 per mile. The number I did see was 3:47. I chuckled under my breath, remembering something Josh Cox said to me on the top floor of the Hilton two days ago: *Dude, it's going to feel like you're jogging.* It did.

A stranger pulled up next to me on the side opposite Alex.

"Are you Matt?" he asked.

"I am," I said.

"I followed your blog," he said. "Good luck."

"Same to you," I said.

I hit the one-mile mark at 6:02, and it was Coach Ben's words I now recalled. *Try to hit a 6:05. If you don't, try to hit a 6:05. If you don't, try to hit a 6:05.*

This counsel was still echoing in my head when an older, bald-headed runner sidled up beside me.

"I don't mean to bother you, Matt," he said in an Australian accent, "but I just wanted to say how inspired I am by what you're doing. Good luck today."

"Same to you," I said, beginning to wish myself invisible.

Just then Matthew Centrowitz glided by on my left. A monosyllabic bark of amused surprise—"Ha!"—shot out of my mouth. Alex and two or three others, also recognizing him, took off after the reigning Olympic champion at 1500 meters (who was clearly having a lark, not actually competing) to clap him on the back and trade fist bumps. My wish had been granted: as long as Centro remained nearby, I was indeed invisible.

By two miles (12:10), the initial crush of bodies had loosened up considerably. No longer worried about accidental collisions, I lowered my eyes to the road, tracking the blue tangent line I learned about in yesterday's technical meeting. When we came upon the first drink station, my fellow 6:05-per-milers scrambled to the margins of the street for cups while I continued to hew to the blue line, knowing the first elite fluid station was coming up at 5K. So absorbed was my attention in the ground in front of me that I failed to notice James's presence at three miles (18:16) until his familiar baritone boomed over the shrill chorus of spectators surrounding him.

"Let's go, Matt!" he bellowed through cupped hands. "Looking smooth."

Ahead, in the dead center of the road, I spied the promised arrangement of folding tables, its display of plastic drink containers picked over like a grocery store canned goods aisle the day before a hurricane, making my blue Hoka bottle that much easier to find, just as I'd hoped. I snatched it up and took my time drinking the 8.5 ounces it contained, even unscrewing the lid to get the last swallow that, I knew from practice, would not come out by squeezing. When the bottle was empty, I tossed it to the side of the road.

Our northward march continued, through Near North, Old Town Triangle, Lincoln Park. I saw nothing but a blue line in any of these diverse neighborhoods. Dance music, pulsing through powerful outdoor speakers, registered briefly at a deep layer of my consciousness, but within twenty seconds of the sound's fading behind me I couldn't have said which song it was. My surroundings simply did not exist for me except as a source of mission-critical information, such as wind direction. Whenever the many-turned racecourse directed me into the breeze, I quickly tucked in behind another runner.

At the 10K elite aid station I discovered that some other runner had made off with my second drink bottle, one of my greatest fears coming into the race.

"Fuck!" I cussed, drawing a sidelong glance from Alex, who had come back to me after his freak-out over Centro.

Knowing I could not afford to go another 5K without fluid or calories, I grabbed two cups of Gatorade from the next regular aid station, swallowing about one cup's worth and feeling the rest soak through my shirtfront.

Stay positive, I told myself. *It could be worse.*

And then it was. Approaching eight miles (48:35), I felt a sudden tug on the left side of my groin—a sickening harbinger of impending doom, like a 2:00 A.M. phone call. Forget the missing drink bottle: *This* was my greatest fear, the one thing that could ruin everything. Outwardly, nothing changed; my body kept moving southward at a steady 9.9 miles per hour. But inside, my emotional state was like the interior of a mine-struck submarine, sirens wailing, drowning men screaming, water level rising. With eighteen miles of hard running left ahead of me, there was only one way this thing could go, and no amount of positive thinking could change it.

Sure enough, over the next mile the tug became a pull, the pull a yank. I felt my entire body tensing, bracing for the now-inevitable nail-gun shot. Seeing his chance, my inner wimp seized control of my thoughts, and I began to halfway welcome the coming showstopper, the sudden blast of pain that would send me lurching to the curb. At least it would spare me the agony of falling short without excuse.

When the pain leveled off—at least for the moment—during Mile 9, I was almost disappointed. My inner wimp went hunting for other ways to let me off the hook. What if I backed off just a little and sort of coasted to a time in the low-2:41 range? I would still come away with a personal record! My fake pro runner experiment would still be a success! Other runners would still be inspired!

Try as I might, I couldn't convince myself that any of this was true. Two thirty-nine was the number in my heart and had been for fifteen years. The only thing that had changed was that I now felt the full weight of the pressure I had placed on myself to claim that yearned-for figure at long last, in what was surely my very last chance.

I came to the 15K elite fluid station. The first table—my table—was not only completely cleared of bottles but being packed away by a couple of race staffers, one at each end. Sensing my approach, the guy facing me looked up, his eyes widening at the sight of my red (elite) number bib. I spread my arms, palms upturned, miming the question etched on my slack-jawed face: *Dude, what the hell?* He replied with a nonapologetic shrug whose meaning was equally plain: *Tough luck, old-timer.*

Shadowed by Alex, I passed ten miles at 1:00:50, still on pace, right down to the tenth of a second. But I saw the glass half empty, interpreting this number not as an indicator of perfect execution but as a warning that I had no margin to slip.

A pair of twenty-something runners, obviously buddies, one tattooed, the other bearded, caught us from behind, their approach heralded by snatches of conversation between them. *Great,* I thought. *More chatterboxes.*

"What time are you shooting for?" the bearded one asked us.

Shut up and leave me alone.

"Under two forty," Alex said.

My stomach clenched. The goal that I had coveted for so long and been so confident of achieving as recently as two hours ago now seemed an onerous outside imposition, an impossible demand forced upon me by a person I no longer was.

On the road ahead a strip of rubber with the look of an ineffectually low speed bump appeared—a timing mat marking the halfway point of the race. All four of us dipped our heads toward our wrists as we passed over it, my watch reading 1:19:41.

"We're doing it!" said the tattooed guy.

This time Alex, too, kept his peace, and a runner's sixth sense told me he was beginning to struggle. For some reason this made me feel better, as though Alex's loss were my gain. My pace lifted ever so slightly, and before I knew it my unwanted companions were behind me. I caught and passed another runner and then found myself blessedly alone again, the nearest competitor a full block in front of me on ruler-straight Adams Street. At fourteen miles, I stole another glance at my wrist and discovered I'd completed the preceding mile in 5:58, my fastest of the race. It was then I realized I wasn't the least bit tired, something my groin crisis and my missed bottles had kept me from noticing before. Seizing the opportunity, my inner hero shoved aside my inner wimp and regained control of my thoughts.

You can do this.

I ran the next mile in 6:04 (finding my 25K drink bottle right where it belonged) and the next in six minutes flat. With the pain in my hurt tendon still holding steady and fatigue encroaching as slowly as summer shadows lengthen, I went back to plan A and began to think about "squeezing down," as Coach Ben called it. His instruction had been to hang fire until at least 30K and then assess my capacity to attack. At the 30K elite aid station (1:53:14), I grabbed the special bottle in which I'd dissolved a caffeine tablet in my drink, gulped it down, tossed the empty, and increased my speed by the smallest perceivable increment.

My groin seized instantly, like a stone-weighted rope snapping taut. I backed off and the twinge subsided. *Now what?* My split time for Mile 19, a comfortable 6:01, decided the question. I gave it another go, but the tendon grabbed again, a final warning.

This was torture. Never had I felt so strong so late in a marathon. I *knew* I could go faster, except I couldn't, all thanks to a single mutinous worm of connective tissue. I felt a mad urge to punish it somehow, but that was impossible—and mad—so I dug my fingernails into my palms instead.

Out of nowhere, one of my earliest memories came to me, one I hadn't thought about in years, and hardly the first I would have expected to pop into my head at such a moment. I was three years old, maybe four, and I had recently developed a fear of going to bed. Night after night I begged my mom not to leave me alone, and she would sit at the edge of my twin mattress with the Looney Tunes sheets and gently enquire into the source of my fear, but I wouldn't reveal it, not wanting to be judged silly or babyish. Eventually, though, Mom's patience coaxed me into confessing I was afraid the moon would fall on my head, a notion I'd picked up from the illustrations in my favorite book, *Goodnight Moon.* Mom assured me the moon wasn't like the balls I played with; it had hung in the sky for a very long time and would never fall. I believed her, and my fear vanished.

I've been a striver all my life, driven by an achievement complex that grew out of my relationship with my father, who, in my formative years, took such obvious delight in my successes in our shared passions of running and writing that I came to crave success insatiably. Why have I wanted so badly for so long to complete a marathon in less than two hours and forty minutes? For many reasons, none of them bad, but the reason behind all the reasons is to make daddy proud. His love for me is unconditional, I know, but it is my mother more than any other person whose love has made me feel okay just as I am: afraid sometimes, imperfect always, an out-and-out failure oftentimes.

And now, suddenly, *this* was okay—completing the Chicago Marathon a little bit slower than I felt I ought to because of one faulty piece of me. At twenty miles (2:01:43) I did some mental math and determined that I needed to run the closing 10K at 6:09 per mile or better to achieve my goal, and I couldn't imagine failing to do so given how the rest of me felt, so I decided then to let the remaining miles be a celebration. Who says the last part of the best marathon you've ever run can't be a cakewalk? *You've earned this,* I told myself. *Enjoy it.*

A female runner overtook me, looking even better than I felt. My competitive instincts rose up, but I tamped them down and let her go. Sooner than seemed possible, the 23 mile sign was behind me. Having covered the preceding 5K in 19:03, I now had 19 minutes and 14 seconds, a goddamn eternity, to complete the next and last 5K. I could practically walk from here, it seemed. My confidence was absolute.

"Let's go, Fitz!" shrieked a familiar voice from my left. "One more mile! You've got this!"

It was Jen Rosario—just one of the many Flagstaff friends who had invested in my dream in ways and to a degree that exceeded my highest hopes. *Run one mile for each of us,* Futsum had enjoined. Only now did I fully appreciate what my teammate had meant by these words, how much I owed to him and the others.

Turning my attention back to the road, I spied a lone figure striding far ahead on Michigan Avenue, at the very horizon of my field of vision. Even at this distance I knew the wide-elbowed arm swing, the trailing brown mane. Sarah Crouch, my quasi-rival, clearly hurting. I knew I wouldn't catch her—the math was against it—nor did I really want to. If she finished even a minute ahead of me, she'd have had a poor race by her standards, and racing is her meal ticket, not mine. Sarah had believed in me more than I myself had, more than anyone outside of Nataki, who in her innocence thought I could beat Feyisa Lilesa; I could live with whatever gloating she might subject me to later.

I passed under a banner marking 800 meters to the finish line and did another calculation. Three minutes left in a running experience I would never equal. I wanted these three minutes to last forever, willed my senses to savor them into permanence, to not just hear the thickening crowd's roar but to record it, to not just feel the triumph of fitness over fatigue in my legs but to brand this feeling onto my brain's memory banks.

Right on Roosevelt. Left on Columbus. The finish line. Crossing it, I raised my arms in victory, as Galen Rupp had done precisely half an hour before when he broke the tape. I had completed the 2017 Chicago Marathon in 144th place, fourth among runners my age and older, dead last in the men's pro division, in an official time of 2:39:30. My average pace over the full distance was 6:05.005 per mile. I felt a single emotion: relief.

Noting my red bib, a race official directed me to an usher, a local high-school kid, whose job was to guide pro finishers to the VIP recovery tent. The very first person I saw when I got there was Aaron Braun, seated in a folding chair in a grassy area outside the tent and talking to Annika, who stood on the other side of a security fence.

"How did you do?" he called out to me.

I spoke the number, and that's when it became real. A gush of purest, first-kiss ecstasy washed away my mere relief. Too good to be true, yet true! How many moments of this description does any human being get to experience in seven to nine decades of mortal existence? Here and now for me was one.

"Damn! You beat me!"

At dinner yesterday Aaron and I had made a friendly wager: drinks on him if he finished less than twenty-eight minutes ahead of me, drinks on me if he matched or exceeded this handicap. I passed through the tent and took a seat beside my teammate (former teammate?), who had passed a most interesting morning, I now learned, leading the race through almost the entire first half and in the process earning himself the moniker "the Flagstaff Flash" on the television broadcast. When the race broke open at fourteen miles, Brauny fell back, suffering mightily over the final twelve miles, yet he hung on to finish twelfth with a time of 2:13:41. He'd placed third among American runners and beaten a number of big names, including Diego Estrada and Feyisa Lilesa. For his pains, he'd earned $16,500.

Coach Ben joined us just as Aaron was wrapping up his narrative, having walked over from the 40K point of the racecourse.

"You did it!" he said, raising a palm for a high five. I left him hanging and wrapped my coach (former coach?) in a sweaty embrace.

Josh Cox appeared next and led us over to a waiting golf cart, another perk of the pro experience. In no time we were back at the Hilton, where yet another clipboard bearing race staffer checked Aaron's and my names off a list, freeing us to attack a buffet that had been set up in the same room we ate dinner in yesterday the final perk. While we ate, we made plans to eat again after Brauny and I got cleaned up. Having a lot more ground to cover than the others did, I rose first and departed, trying to decide on the best way to get to the Hotel Chicago. Realizing my legs felt pretty decent, I decided to run.

Outside, on a sidewalk choked with supporters of runners still out on the course, I eased into a cautious trot, assessing my aches and pains. At nine minutes per mile, they were minimal, so I continued, placing a call to my parents as I weaved between human obstacles.

"I saw you on TV!" my dad said.

Mom had forgotten I was running a marathon today but was pleased that I was pleased. My time meant nothing to her.

In my room, I stripped off my uniform and was just about to step into the shower when I caught a glimpse of my body in the bathroom mirror. Sorrow hit me like a rogue wave as I regarded my veiny, whippet-like physique—not a beautiful body, perhaps, but a body more beautifully adapted to the challenge of long-distance running than it had ever been before or would ever be again. Tomorrow I would look a little less like this reflected image, the next day a little less.

Within an hour, as if determined to hasten this degenerative process, I was gobbling french fries and throwing back beers with the NAZ Elite crew at First Draft, Josh Cox in full Jerry Maguire mode, negotiating with the manager for better seating, paying for everything. Aaron was in high spirits and already tipsy, showing a side of himself I hadn't so much as glimpsed previously. At two o'clock, Ben, Jen, and Addison left to catch a flight. Josh settled the tab and split as well. Out on the sidewalk, Brauny fixed me with a beseeching look.

"What do you want to do now?" he said.

"I figured I'd head back to my hotel," I said. "I need to make some phone calls and catch up on social media."

Congratulations had been pouring in. Matt, Big Dog, Monica, AJ, Shannon, Too Slow, Rochelle—pretty much everyone I knew in Flagstaff had patted my back in one electronic form or another.

"I want to keep drinking!" Brauny implored.

We agreed to meet up for dinner with his parents. I had no intention of flaking, but after talking to Nataki and my brothers and responding to all the texts and tweets and Facebook comments, I felt myself beginning to fade, so I texted Brauny to request a rain check. His reply came so swiftly that I half wondered if he hadn't typed it out in advance and only needed to hit SEND.

Ah man, coming off of that high? I still need to buy you a drink! Or three!

Guilt and exhaustion waged a pitched battle inside my mind. Exhaustion won, and I began to script a polite, yet firm final refusal, but before I could get it off, Brauny texted again.

Rally Buddy! Try to rally!

The inner battle was renewed, but this time guilt had an ally in the form of the thought that I might never have another opportunity like this. I mean, how often does a top professional athlete in your favorite sport beg you to get drunk with him?

Me: Aw, screw it. I'm coming.

Aaron: YES!!!

Fifteen minutes later, I joined Aaron and Annika, their daughters, Aaron's parents, and Sarah Cotton at Cantina Laredo. Having already eaten all my stomach could hold, I drank a margarita while the others dug into enchiladas and quesadillas. When the bill was paid, the grandparents took Mackenzie and Myla back to their hotel and the rest of us set out in search of more alcohol, bar hopping until well past midnight, parting with a round of boozy embraces at the corner of Grand and Lasalle. I had rallied all right, to the point where I hadn't wanted the night to end any more than Brauny, though not entirely for the same reasons. At thirty, he was celebrating a new beginning, eyes on the future, whereas I was marking a completion, looking back one last time before closing the door.

During the short walk to my hotel, I caught a glimpse of a gibbous moon floating above the rooftops.

"Goodnight, moon," I said.

RETIREMENT

October 9, 2017

Way too early (as Kellyn Taylor would say) on the morning after the 2017 Chicago Marathon, Coach Ben, who was already back in Flagstaff, joined me on a call with Final Surge podcast host Dean Oullette to discuss my now-completed adventures as a fake pro runner.

"So, what's next for you, Matt?" Dean asked at the tail end of the hour-long interview. "Are you going to go after a personal best in the mile?"

My throat issued a gravelly rattle that started as a laugh and turned into a cough, sending daggers through my throbbing brain.

"No, I think that would be a mistake," I said. "This has been a truly magical experience, but it wasn't meant to last forever. Now I just want to take a step back from running, give away some fitness, and prioritize my work and my wife and some other things. I'm always going to be an athlete, but I don't want to try to hang on to yesterday. I'll let the next goal come to me on its own time, and it will probably be something very different from a personal best attempt in the mile."

Aaron and I caught the same flight out of O'Hare a few hours later, landing at Pulliam around five in the afternoon and parting at baggage claim with plans to meet up again the same evening for a little hair of the dog. Nataki picked me up curbside in the Fun Mobile and squired me back to Matt's house, where I stepped through the front door to find a congratulatory helium balloon floating above the dining room table, its string tethered to a clear-plastic takeout container with a hunk of chocolate-peanut butter cake inside. Silent at first, the room suddenly exploded into sound, thumping club music issuing from a wireless speaker positioned near the

500-calorie reward, and in the next instant the orchestrator of my home-coming surprise popped out from his hiding place in the kitchen, arms outspread and that Pepsodent smile lighting up his face. I gave Matt a double high five followed by a hearty embrace. As we stepped back from each other, his face assumed an expectant expression, an apparent invitation to say a few words. Unprepared, I spoke the only words that came to me.

"Well, I didn't blow it!"

When the sun rose the next morning, Nataki and I were already hustling to get our stuff packed ahead of the team's arrival at Matt's place to bid us farewell and then get on with their young lives, running together up to Fort Tuthill while we embarked on the long drive back to reality. With novelistic symmetry, Faubs was the first NAZ Elite member to appear. I met him in the driveway, in a familiar pose, kneeling on an exercise mat with a rubber strap looped around his knee.

"So, what's next for you?" he asked, repeating Dean Willett's question from the day before. "Boston? London?"

"Nah, I'm retired," I said. "I'm not even thinking about other races right now."

"Seriously? You're not going to do another marathon?"

"Oh, I'm sure I will," I said. "Just not anytime soon."

The rest of the team (minus Aaron, who was sleeping in) rolled in while Scott and I chatted. Ben Bruce strode toward me purposefully with a gift bag in hand. I plunged a forearm into it and withdrew a long-sleeve NAZ Elite top in powder blue wrapped around a bottle of imperial stout.

"That's a strong one," he cautioned.

Coach Ben passed around a Sharpie and an eight-by-ten print of the photo Jen had taken of me with the team the week before and everyone signed it.

"How's your body feeling?" Kellyn asked, scribbling her name as close to her image as she could get it.

"Fine," I said. "I could probably run now if I had to."

"That means you didn't race hard enough."

Receiving the autographed print back from its final signatory, Futsum, Coach Ben stuffed it inside a simple frame and presented it to me with touching formality.

"I know I speak for the whole team when I say it was an honor and a pleasure to have you with us these last thirteen weeks," he said. "You brought a lot of positive energy to the group and I hope your example stays with us as we move forward."

"I can't believe *you're* thanking *me!*" I said. "All of you have given me so much—more than I'll ever be able to repay. I just hope the story I tell rewards you in some small way. I promise I'm a better writer than I am a runner!"

"Oh, I'm sure your book will be two thirty-eight material, at least," Ben Bruce said drily.

I hugged everyone and then watched as my (now undeniably) former teammates shuffled away in a loose pack, descending toward Pullman Drive, crossing over to the far sidewalk, and bending left to begin the ascent to the park, my eyes fixed on their backs until they were out of sight, just in case someone glanced behind and gave me a final wave, but no one did.

Nataki and I had been home for all of two weeks when, against my stated intentions, I abandoned my plan to put running on the back burner for a while and signed up for a spring marathon in New Orleans, convinced I could exceed my Chicago performance— despite a few more gray hairs with better weather and a more cooperative left hip abductor tendon. In pursuit of this, I replicated as much of my Flagstaff formula as I could (purchasing the NAZ Elite Advanced Marathon Plan from Final Surge, keeping up with my form drills and rehab exercises) and did without the rest (coaching, altitude, endless trails, teammates, weekly sports massage, daily physical therapy, a sports psychologist, etc.).

Things went okay at first. In mid-December I won a local 5K, proving I hadn't lost everything I'd gained in Flagstaff, but two weeks later I hurt my groin again, and that was the end of that. Lacking access to AJ Gregg and his cold laser, I was still less than fully healed in July, when Nataki and I made our first visit to Flagstaff since we left, fulfilling a promise I'd made to return for Stephanie and Ben Bruce's running camp (as a regular paying customer this time).

Retracing the same route we took the year before, we arrived just in time for a 6:30 dinner date with James McKirdy and Heather Szuba, who were now living in Flagstaff full-time and engaged to be married.

"So, how does it feel to be back?" James asked me after a toast to friendship.

"Honestly, kind of painful," I said. "When we were cruising along the strip just now I felt this hopeless yearning to go back in time and do it all again."

James and Heather's relocation and betrothal were not the only changes that had occurred since Nataki and I had been away. Eric Fernandez was now married to Angela Gavelli and making strides in his new career as a financial planner. Craig Lutz, Rochelle Kanuho, and Matt Llano were no longer members of NAZ Elite, Craig having moved to Santa Barbara, where he worked as a marketing intern for Hoka; Rochelle remaining in her native Flagstaff but training on her own without a coach or a sponsor; and Matt still struggling to regain his 2014 form against a litany of recent diagnoses—asthma, severe allergies, something called paradoxical vocal chord dysfunction—and a small but scary setback with his surgically repaired left hip. Ben Bruce had transitioned into an assistant coaching role but was still racing a bit, his abdominal injury having turned out to be something else entirely. ("Joke's on me," he wrote in an email. "I asked you if you broke your penis and meanwhile I was running on a fractured pelvis.") To offset the attrition, Coach Ben had added a quartet of talented young women to the team, including Kenyan expatriate Aliphine Tuliamuk, whose bar-raising presence had helped push Kellyn Taylor and Stephanie Bruce to new heights, Kellyn becoming the seventh-fastest American woman marathoner in history with a 2:24:28 victory at Grandma's Marathon in June and Steph winning her first national championship title three weeks later at the Peachtree Road Race in Atlanta. Unsurprisingly, Kellyn had also passed her firefighter test on her second attempt.

Travel weary, Nataki and I declined dessert and parted from James and Heather with vague plans to meet up again before we returned to California, then made straight for the local Best Western. When I woke up it was Thursday, a day I started as though I had never left Flagstaff, showing up unannounced at the Bagel Run, not to participate (I wanted to spare my groin for camp) but to have Aaron Braun sign the team photo he'd been unable to endorse on my last morning in Flagstaff. Three hours later, sticking to my former routine, I crashed the NAZ Elite team strength workout at Hypo2, where AJ Gregg, just like old times, pointed out a fault in my side plank technique. And my single-leg reverse deadlift technique. And my kettlebell swing technique.

"Are those the same cargo shorts you had last summer?" Faubs asked as I slipped them back on after the workout.

"They are indeed," I said. "I'm flattered you noticed."

Continuing the nostalgia tour, Nataki and I stopped for lunch at Kickstand Kafé, where we made a spur-of-the-moment decision to ambush Matt at his house. Having lived with him for thirteen weeks, we knew the timing was good, our 12:45 p.m. arrival falling in a gap between First Run and Nap in Matt's normal Thursday routine.

A stranger—tall, slender, twenty-something, with a blond pompadour—answered the door. He gawked at us, and we at him, in mutual surprise, his expression reflecting my thought: *Who the hell are you?* Then Matt appeared behind the young man, gripping Harlow's collar tightly in both hands. Tail wagging, Queenie's old walking buddy whined and strained after us, remembering our scent, if not our faces.

"Come on in!" Matt said, grinning at 2,000 lumens. "We were just having lunch."

We followed our onetime host back to the kitchen, where he picked up the bowl of grilled Sriracha salmon, roasted Brussels sprouts and sweet potatoes, and faro he'd set down when the doorbell chimed and introduced us to the pompadoured stranger, whose name was Brannon and who was Matt's boyfriend. The couple had met in February, which, by sheer coincidence, was around the time Matt's health issues had begun. Since then his personal and professional lives had traveled in opposite directions: Matt fell in love, ran a series of mediocre races, invited Brannon to move in with him, quit NAZ Elite, and now had no idea what his next step was.

"I've gotten really into quotations lately," he told us. "Recently I found one that I'm really hanging on to: 'When it seems like things are falling apart, they may actually be falling into place.'"

Ben and Steph's camp followed the same itinerary as the year before, kicking off with an afternoon run at Buffalo Park—a run I'd been forced to skip in 2017, having injured my groin the previous day. Refusing to sit it out a second time, I completed a single two-mile loop at the back of the group. This went better than expected, so the next morning I ran 4.7 miles with my fellow campers at Hart Prairie, elevation 8,500 feet. Surprised again by the tendon's quiescence, I ran 12 miles at Woody Mountain Road on Saturday, accompanied by volunteer camp counselor Bob Tusso, who, despite having completed a 27-mile trail race with 4,000 feet of elevation gain just six days earlier, was, as always, up for anything. I felt unaccountably good—not merely pain-free but also 100 percent comfortable at a pace that wasn't a heck of a lot slower than I'd averaged in my last long run on Woody Mountain Road, a week before Chicago.

"This place just suits me, man," I told Too Slow. "I can't explain it."

That night we all gathered in Kellyn's backyard for pizza, beer, a bonfire, s'mores, and a goal-setting exercise. I found Kellyn standing sentinel on the back patio, guarding the home's rear entrance from unwelcome ingress by her guests, who weren't really her guests at all but Ben and Steph's.

"Thanks for letting us hang out at your place," I said apologetically.

"You're welcome," Kellyn said. "I love people."

The faintest hint of a smile crooked the corners of her lips, confirming something I had always suspected about Kellyn—namely, that although her prickly personality is no act, she is perfectly aware of how it plays, and is not unwilling to have a little fun with it on occasion.

"We'll be out of here by eight," I promised.

Steph appeared quietly at my side. She'd been going a mile a minute since camp began and I hadn't had much time with her.

"I've been meaning to ask you how your mom is doing," she said, lowering her voice.

I gave her a queasy look, which Steph mirrored.

"What can I say?" I said. "It's a degenerative disease, and it's taking its course. But I've been visiting her and my dad every six or eight weeks since I left Flagstaff, and that's been good. Something you and Ben said to me on the day I learned about her diagnosis has stuck with me—that happy moments matter even if they aren't remembered."

Steph placed a hand on my shoulder and gave it a comforting squeeze.

When everyone had eaten their fill of pizza, Ben kicked off the more formal part of the evening's agenda by reading some remarks that Coach Ben (who was vacationing with his family in St. Louis) had written for the occasion.

"Hey, guys, sorry I couldn't be with you in person tonight," he began. "I was able to make it last year and I had a blast, so I wanted at least to have Steph and Ben share a few thoughts with you."

Ben raised his eyes from his phone to his audience, as if to measure our interest. Appearing satisfied, he resumed.

"Show of hands: Who here has a running goal or goals of some kind?"

Twenty-three arms shot up (twenty-five if you counted 2016 Olympian Jared Ward and 2018 U.S. 5000-meter national championship runner-up Rachel Schneider, who had given talks earlier in the day).

"Okay," Ben Bruce continued on Coach Ben's behalf. "Now pare it down to your number-one goal. Raise your hand if that goal is associated with a time."

An almost equal number of arms were lifted.

"Keep your hand raised if that time is one of the following," Ben read: "a Boston qualifying time or a round number (meaning something that ends in a zero). I'm not there, but I'll bet there are a lot of hands up."

This was true.

"Okay, hands back down," Ben went on. "We'll do one more: Raise your hand if your goal is *not* associated with a time at all. Anyone? Again, I am not there, but I'm guessing there are probably fewer than five hands up."

Ben paused to count. There were exactly five.

"That's not a bad thing," Ben read. "I'm not going to yell at all of you who have time goals. But I do think they can be a little bit arbitrary, and

I want to explore a couple of alternatives and get you thinking about your running in a different way."

Realizing that permission to drop their hands was not forthcoming, the five who still held them aloft did so by their own initiative.

"It occurred to me at the beginning of this year," Ben read on, "that, on our team, the last thing we needed to worry about was ambition. All of our athletes had packed up and moved to Flagstaff from wherever they called home in order to pursue their dreams. This was as motivated a group of people as I'd ever known. Sitting down and talking about tangible goals—two twenty-five for a marathon for the women or two ten for a marathon for the men—wasn't something we really needed to do. Winning national titles also wasn't something we needed to talk about. Making the Olympic team wasn't even something we needed to talk about. What I realized was that, if and when these things happened, they would simply be the byproduct of what, at our core, we all want to do in this sport, which is to find out how good we can really be. Since that time I've tried to focus on working with each athlete on something that seems simple: just getting better, one training segment at a time. Just being as fit as possible."

Ben paused again to make sure we hadn't all fallen asleep on him before forging ahead.

"And you know what happens when you do that? Instead of *chasing* the fitness, the fitness *comes to* you. And you know what else? It's more fun. My high-school coach called it 'enjoying the process.' Now, I won't make you raise your hands again, but I would bet an awful lot of money [here Ben Bruce inserted an aside about Ben Rosario's affinity for gaming] that there are plenty of you sitting there who start each training segment, whether it's twelve weeks, twenty weeks, or even a whole year out from your goal race, with a very tangible goal in mind. And I'll bet that same amount that there are plenty of you who've done this only to become frustrated because you're not hitting the times in practice that some chart says you should be hitting if you want to run that particular time. Am I right?"

Suddenly my mind flew back to last year's bonfire. On that occasion, Steph asked each camper to write down three goals—a modest "C" goal, a more ambitious "B" goal, and an audacious "A" goal—on an index card and share them with the group. Unable to run at the time, I told my fellow campers that my "C" goal was to find a way to still race the Chicago Marathon in seven weeks. My "B" goal was, as I put it, "to run my fastest marathon since my fastest marathon," which meant beating the time of 2:49:14 I'd run in Eugene in May. And my "A" goal was "to achieve something on the streets of Chicago that makes everyone here believe they can achieve *their* 'A' goal." To me, this meant running 2:39, though I kept the number to myself, having not yet shared it with anyone.

One year later, as I listened to my former teammate deliver my former coach's sermon on goal setting, I was struck by how deeply and uniquely human is this business of setting and chasing goals. It speaks, I think, to the ever-striving, never-satisfied, "to boldly go" nature of our kind. In setting and chasing goals we make the meaningless meaningful, the unimportant important. One does not set a goal to reap a good harvest or survive a harsh winter. These are things we simply *must* do. Rather, one sets a goal to sing at the Metropolitan Opera House or to have a paper published in *The New England Medical Journal*. Such nonutilitarian ambitions blur the line between play and real life, making play serious and real life playful. Does it really matter to sing at the Met or to have a paper published in *NEMJ*? Not if survival is all that matters. But if what matters is whatever we *decide* matters, whatever we choose to imbue with meaning, however far removed from mere survival it may be, then yes, these things do matter to those who hook their aspirations to them.

It's a risky enterprise. Far safer is it to remain content with merely getting by. Chasing goals is hard work and often disappointing. There is also the risk of losing perspective, forgetting that, whereas it's always preferable to achieve a goal, it's better to have tried and failed than to have never tried. But as long as you can keep things in perspective, acting as though your very life depends on some semi-arbitrary number may lead you to a richer, more intense and textured experience of life than you would have had otherwise. I know it did for me, at least for the span of one enchanted summer in the autumn of my life.

The sound of my name jolted me out of these reflections.

"I'll pick on Matt Fitzgerald for a second," said Ben Bruce, still reading on behalf of Coach Ben. "One, because I know he can take it, and two, because he's a perfect example."

Twenty-five heads turned in my direction as the present Ben returned to the absent Ben's prepared remarks.

"Last summer Matt came to Flagstaff to train with our group for the Chicago Marathon. He and I sat down and talked about the training he had been doing over the last couple of years so I could understand the context of where he was coming from and what he may or may not be able to handle as we prepared for Chicago. From the beginning, he was pushing to run workout times that would 'prove' he was getting close to two forty shape. But I resisted basing his workout times on those I thought a two forty guy could run, because I didn't think he was a two forty guy—yet. Instead, I just wanted to see him hit workouts based on his current fitness, and then, if those became too easy (and they did), I'd write slightly faster workouts.

"It wasn't until about three weeks out from the race that I thought he was in sub-two forty shape, and it had nothing to do with the fact that it was his dream goal. It's just that his workouts showed me that's what he was capable of. But I think, or at least I hope, that when I finally told him I thought he could run under two forty, it really meant something to him because I had been honest with him throughout the entire training segment. And guess what he ran in Chicago: 2:39:30—a PR at the age of forty-six!"

Someone whistled.

"But the moral of the story isn't even his time," Ben Bruce read. "It's this—and I'll risk all my hypothetical money once again by asking Matt if I'm right. I'll bet that now, one year later, it's not the two thirty-nine next to his name that means the most to Matt. I'll bet it is the memories of the training sessions on Lake Mary Road, the camaraderie of meeting the group every morning, and the feeling he had coming down Michigan Avenue, knowing he was as fit as he had ever been in his life, that mean the most. Because Matt really and truly enjoyed the process when he was here. Matt: Am I right?"

There was a moment of silence as I searched for my voice.

"More than you know, Coach," I said. "More than you know."